VALUES

of the

WISE

~

<u>PROFOUND &</u>
<u>WITTY WORDS OF</u>
<u>WISDOM</u>
<u>FROM THE</u>
<u>GREATEST MINDS</u>

ISBN 0-7414-1399-X

Cover design by Jason Merchey & Chris A. Master

Published by:

PUBLISHING.COM

519 West Lancaster Avenue
Haverford, PA 19041-1413
Info@buybooksontheweb.com
www.buybooksontheweb.com
Toll-free (877) BUY BOOK
Local Phone (610) 520-2500
Fax (610) 519-0261

Printed in the United States of America

Printed on Recycled Paper

Published February 2003

Wisdom: The Charmed Life

This book is about utilizing thinking to lead a more joyous, fulfilling and moral life. Some people think a good life is about money, or power, or progeny. That may be *the* good life, but not a good life. This book expounds the ideals of the ancient Greek philosophers, who believed that understanding is the surest way for one to live in a way such that life is – I will be intentionally vague -- *better*.

My hope is that one will use this accessible and challenging book as an inspirational reference and tool to kick-start pondering a topic of interest. I hope that virtually any one quotation could be lifted out of the context of its chapter and spur thinking in the reader. Optimally, however, one would choose a chapter of interest and slowly digest it in its entirety. This would ideally give the reader a full picture of what I found to be the most compelling thoughts on record about the value in question. The values are arranged around fifteen themes.

Aspiring to the values and ideals of a good life begins with wisdom. For more on wisdom, read on! It is a product of sustained critical thinking and experience. By sensitizing oneself to a deeper way of viewing the world, and especially one's fellow human beings, one can literally live a different life than one was before insight. Thus, simply changing one's thinking changes the whole world, in a way.

To pursue the maturity that wisdom engenders not only makes life more vivid and valuable; perhaps it also makes life easier. To move beyond the small issues of bill-paying, work stress, and whether one wants this or that car may actually make life simpler, like bringing a target into focus and releasing the arrow. There is a quiet but clear reward for living honestly and morally. However, philosopher Denis Diderot called us out centuries ago: "Virtue is praised but hated. People run away from it, for it is ice-cold, and in this world you must keep your feet warm." For more on morality, read on!

I have an interest in wisdom for enlightenment as well as its therapeutic benefits; raw information does not have the potential to change one's life. It can be taken one step further – to predict, assuage, and connect us. However, it takes dedication to keep one's axe to the wheel, so to speak, and *think*. Whether or not it is worth the effort is an individual decision. For more on dedication, read on!

My main part in this work was to assemble thousands of the most compelling thoughts from the finest minds throughout recorded history (admittedly, with a Western bias) to weigh in on the debate. No offense is meant toward women by transcribing many of the quotations as I found them: with in the male pronouns "he," "mankind," etc..

I am honored to be able to play even the role of scribe to the incredible minds featured in this work. The wisdom of countless *great spirits* throughout the ages would dissipate with the wind were it not for the preservation of their insights in the pages of books. For more on magnanimity, read on!

Please keep in mind that what I was attempting to do was to provide all the best evidence in favor of the value the chapter extols. To quote Hitler does not mean that I approve of his actions. Rather, I quote him to elucidate the nature of his belief system, in the hopes that by doing so the reader will be better able to determine not only what they believe, but why. For more on education, read on!

Developing the chapter headings and title, pondering potential quotes, and transcribing the quotations was a special avocation that provided me with pleasure and meaning for years. Quotations and poetry without a citation are original.

I am honored you chose this book. I think you will not be disappointed.

Jason Merchey

ACKNOWLEDGEMENTS

Who I am today is inextricably bound to my circle of family, friends, and others. I would like to thank my mother, who primarily raised me and is originally responsible for the trajectory on which I have been for three decades. I offer appreciation to my father, one of the clear voices of wisdom and morality in my life. My grandma Esther played a tremendous role raising and teaching me.

I owe gratitude and respect to the great minds and notorious charlatans whose words comprise this work. The countless sources from which I have identified these quotations not only provided me with much meaning over the years, but also made this work possible. Sources include conversations, newspaper reports, songs, poetry, lectures, cogitation, compilations, and original works.

I have been substantially influenced by and wish to acknowledge H. Roy Kim, Dustin Beall, David Kim, Kelli Hicks, Arthur Charchian, Kelly Haas, Vanessa Klein, Nhu-Ngoc Ong, David Pierce, Susan Jorgensen, Louis Mone, William Grier, Ambika Talwar, Eric Gruver, P. Chris Cozby, William Puett, Denis Hickey, Sholeh Iravantchi, Cyril Edwards, Jorge Ampudia, Gil Haimson, Karel Placek, Raymond Novaco, Michael E. Kerr, Michael Wellins, Reginald Jones, Bryan Kernal, Jared Donahue, and last, but not least, Johnny "Ringo" Marshall. I also wish to thank Katie Copeland, Melise Blakeslee, and Carole Harris for their special assistance.

I have special thanks for my guide in the publication and publicity process, Penny C. Sansevieri of BooksbyPen.com. I recognize H. Roy Kim for his assistance with distilling the long list of values down to 15 chapters.

Last but not least, I wish to acknowledge my stepfather Stanley Westreich – a seeker of wisdom who made my time spent on this book more possible. P.S. pretty good work ethic, eh?!

TABLE OF CONTENTS

DEDICATION, DISCIPLINE & RESPONSIBILITY

The Constitution only guarantees the American people the right to pursue happiness. You have to catch it yourself.

~ Benjamin Franklin

Men at some time are masters of their fates:
The fault, dear Brutus, is not in our stars,
But in ourselves, that we are underlings.

~ William Shakespeare

Even when we know what is right, too often we fail to act. More often we grab greedily for the day, letting tomorrow bring what it will, putting off the unpleasant and unpopular.

~ Bernard M. Baruch

1

All the adversity I've had in my life, all my troubles and obstacles, have strengthened me.... You may not realize it when it happens, but a kick in the teeth may be the best thing in the world for you.

~ Walt Disney

Happy people plan actions, they don't plan results.

~ Dennis Wholey

The best way to escape from a problem is to solve it.

~ Brendan Francis

Love is the active concern for the life and growth of that which we love.

~ Erich Fromm

It is our responsibility to carry on the spirit, bravery, and patriotism of our nation's fallen heroes of 9/11/2001. The world has witnessed our country's strength in a time of great sorrow. Let us use that strength to create a better world for all its people.

~ Carolyn La Pierre

2

I never blame failures – there are too many complicated situations in life, but I am absolutely merciless toward lack of effort.

~ F. Scott Fitzgerald

An element of abstention, of restraint, must into all the finer joys.

~ Vida D. Scudder

The harder you work, the harder it is to surrender.

~ Vince Lombardi

My great mistake, the fault for which I can't forgive myself, is that one day I ceased my obstinate pursuit of my own individuality.

~ Oscar Wilde

It seems to me that any full-grown, mature adult would have a desire to be responsible, to help where he can in a world that needs so very much, that threatens us so very much.

~ Norman Lear

You can hardly make a friend in a year, but you can lose one in an hour.

~ Chinese proverb

Diligence is the Mother of Good luck.

~ Benjamin Franklin

Modesty and unselfishness—these are virtues which men praise—and pass by.

~ Andre Maurois

My father said there are times to sit or stand and be counted;
When good people die, laws become forsaken, books aflame smolder.
There comes a time when our steed must be armored and mounted;
The balance of good and evil rests on our collective shoulders.

Action springs not from thought, but a readiness for responsibility.

~ Dietrich Bonhoeffer

Heroism, the mountaineers say, is endurance for one moment more.

~ George Kennan

The most important thing a father can do for his children is to love their mother.

~ Theodore Hesburgh

With time and patience the mulberry leaf becomes a silk gown.

~ Chinese proverb

A wise man, to accomplish his end, may even carry his foe on his shoulder.

~ Panchatantra

I think and think for months and years. Ninety-nine times, the conclusion is false. The hundredth time I am right.

~ Albert Einstein

Self-respect is the root of discipline: the sense of dignity grows with the ability to say no to oneself.

~ Abraham J. Heschel

It is time in the West to defend not so much human rights as human obligations.

~ Aleksandr Solzhenitsyn

Instead of sitting down satisfied with the efforts we have already made, which is the wish of our enemies, the necessity of the times, more than ever, calls four our utmost circumspection, deliberation, fortitude, and perseverance.

~ Samuel Adams

A reformer is a guy who rides through a sewer in a glass-bottom boat.

~ James L. Walker

Not hammer strokes, but the dance of the water singes the pebbles into perfection.

~ Rabindranath Tagore

Chi Wen Tzu always thought three times before taking action. Twice would have been quite enough.

~ Confucius

The mastery of nature is vainly believed to be an adequate substitute for self-mastery.

~ Reinhold Niebuhr

The immature mind hops from one thing to another; the mature mind seeks to follow through.

~ Harry A. Overstreet

...the lust for comfort, that stealthy thing that enters the house as a guest, and then becomes a host, and then a master.

~ Kahlil Gibran

Life always gets harder toward the summit – As the cold increases, responsibility increases.

~ Friedrich Nietzsche

Children have never been very good at listening to their elders, but they have never failed to imitate them.

~ James Baldwin

Many persons have a wrong idea of what constitutes true happiness. It is not attained through self-gratification but through fidelity to a worthy purpose.

~ Helen Keller

Man's responsibility increases as that of the gods decreases.

~ Andre Gide

Everyone ought to bear patiently the results of his own conduct.

~ Phaedrus

If you won't be better tomorrow than you were today, then what do you need tomorrow for?

~ Rabbi Nahman of Bratslav

Revolution is not a one-time event.

~ Audre Lorde

Here is a test to find whether your mission on earth is finished: If you're alive, it isn't.

~ Richard Bach

Empty is the argument of the philosopher which does not relieve any human suffering.

~ Epicurus

If every desire were satisfied as soon as it arose, how would men occupy their lives, how would they pass the time?

~ Arthur Schopenhauer

Good people are good because they've come to wisdom through failure. We get very little wisdom from success.

~ William Saroyan

He does right, pleasing himself and his counselor
But his decision was not based purely on lofty virtues
Fear, obligations, and pressure muddy the water
If one is forced, did one of his own volition choose?

Members of the left, along with the far larger number
of squishy "progressives," have grossly failed to live
up to their responsibility to think; rather, they are
merely reacting, substituting tired slogans for thought.

~ Christopher Hitchens

We will either find a way, or make one.

~ Hannibal

The harder you work, the luckier you get.

~ Gary Player

To be capable of steady friendship or lasting love are
the two greatest proofs, not only of goodness of heart,
but of strength of mind.

~ William Hazlitt

Every man is the son of his own works.

~ Miguel de Cervantes

Things we bank on can be shattered before our eyes.
Hard work and planning can disintegrate.
Even though we keep our eyes on the prize,
We may be victims of insidious fate.

Whatever a man soweth, that shall he also reap.

~ Paul 6:7

Talk doesn't cook rice.

~ Chinese proverb

The investigation of the meaning of words is the
beginning of education.

~ Antisthenes

After pleasant scratching comes unpleasant itching.

~ Danish proverb

Liberals are very broadminded: they are always willing to give careful consideration to both sides of the same side.

~ Anonymous

We might have been graced with each other,
Only to find ourselves cursed by merciless time.
Perhaps a promising future lay before us~
But it's a towering mountain my heart must climb.

Each partner must systematically subordinate himself or herself to the other. That is the only formula for a happy marriage.

~ John Kenneth Galbraith

If you don't crack the shell, you can't eat the nut.

~ Persian proverb

Life is a series of problems. Do we want to moan about them or solve them?

~ M. Scott Peck

He who cannot love must learn to flatter.

~ Johann Wolfgang von Goethe

Real generosity toward the future lies in giving all to the present.

~ Albert Camus

Pray to God but keep on rowing the boat ashore.

~ Russian proverb

When they turn the pages of history,
When these days have passed long ago,
Will they read of us with sadness,
For the seeds that we let grow?
We turned our gaze from the castles in the distance
Eyes cast down on the path of least resistance...

~ Neil Peart

I may not always have done what was right, but at least I had good intentions.

~ Jean Jacques Rousseau

Few things can help an individual more than to place responsibility upon him, and to let him know that you trust him.

~ Booker T. Washington

Are you on your child's back or his team? Get off his back; get on his team.

~ Howard G. Hendricks

I hope that while so many people are out smelling the flowers, someone is taking the time to plant some.

~ Herbert Rappaport

Discipline is the tool required to solve life's problems. What are these tools, these techniques of suffering, these means of experiencing the pain of problems directly? Delaying gratification, accepting responsibility, dedication to truth, and balance.

~ M. Scott Peck

The price of greatness is responsibility.

~ Winston Churchill

The proper office of a friend is to side with you when you are in the wrong. Nearly anybody will side with you when you are in the right.

~ Mark Twain

There is no such thing as great talent without great willpower.

~ Honore de Balzac

Love provides the motive, the energy for discipline. It is the will to extend oneself for the purpose of nurturing one's own, or another's, spiritual growth.

~ M. Scott Peck

I believe in looking reality straight in the eye and denying it.

~ Garrison Keillor

There is no expedient to which a man will not go to avoid the labor of thinking.

~ Thomas Edison

Love is not effortless; to the contrary, love is effortful.

~ M. Scott Peck

Work saves us from three great evils: boredom, vice and need.

~ Voltaire

What is the use of a house if you haven't got a tolerable planet to put it on?

~ Henry David Thoreau

Effort is only effort when it begins to hurt.

~ Ortega y Gasset

For evil to flourish the good need just stand by and do nothing.
Many "good Christians" and so-called ethical leaders deserve shame.
They turned their heads and turned in their friends to their king;
They rendered the lofty principles of their philosophers lame.

(First line an adapted quote from Elie Wiesel)

Those who fight, bleed, and cry beside me shall also rejoice, sing, and dance with me.

~ David Kim

You really can change the world if you care enough.

~ Marian Wright Edelman

The easiest way for your children to learn about money is for you not to have any.

~ Katharine Whitehorn

You can surrender without a prayer, but never really pray ~ without surrender.
You can fight without ever winning, but never really win ~ without a fight

~ Neil Peart

A philosophical orientation is one thing; it is rewarding if one also has the requisite courage. However, *wondering* to the point of complacency or inaction is quite another.

A conservative is a man who sits and thinks, mostly sits.

~ Woodrow Wilson

There is no moral precept that does not have something inconvenient about it.

~ Denis Diderot

Volunteering is at the very core of being a human. No one has made it through life without someone else's help.

~ Heather French

No problem can withstand the assault of sustained thinking.

~ Voltaire

It is a far, far better thing to have a firm anchor in nonsense than to put out on the troubled sea of thought.

~ John Kenneth Galbraith

Aristotle maintained that women have fewer teeth than men; although he was twice married, it never occurred to him to verify this statement by examining his wives' mouths.

~ Bertrand Russell

Is sloppiness in speech caused by ignorance or apathy? I don't know and I don't care.

~ William Safire

Who is rich? He that is content. Who is that? Nobody.

~ Benjamin Franklin

I can rest only for a moment, for with freedom comes responsibilities, and I dare not linger, for my long walk is not yet ended.

~ Nelson Mandela

The keenest sorrow is to recognize ourselves as the sole cause of all our adversities.

~ Sophocles

Most men pursue pleasure with such breathless haste that they hurry past it.

~ Soren Kierkegaard

Women who seek to be equal with men lack ambition.

~ Timothy Leary

The road to enlightenment is long and narrow.

Adversity introduces a man to himself.

~ Anonymous

If you take too long in deciding what to do with your life, you'll find you've done it.

~ George Bernard Shaw

LIBERTY & PEACE

The time to build is upon us.

~ Nelson Mandela

I believe there are more instances of the abridgement of the freedom of the people by gradual and silent encroachments of those in power than by violent and sudden usurpations.

~ James Madison

America is not violent because of movies. Movies are violent because of America.

~ Ian Kerkhof

Peace is when time doesn't matter as it passes by.

~ Maria Schell

Whatever crushes individuality is despotism, by whatever name it may be called.

~ John Stuart Mill

Patriotism is the willingness to kill and be killed for trivial reasons.

~ Bertrand Russell

The most powerful obstacle to culture... is the tendency to aggression, [which is] an innate, independent, instinctual disposition in man.

~ Sigmund Freud

The master class has always brought a war, and the subject class has always fought the battle.

~ Eugene V. Debs

No system has ever existed which did not in some form involve the exploitation of some human beings for the advantage of others.

~ John Dewey

Most Americans would say they disapproved of violence. But what they really mean is that they believe it should be the monopoly of the state.

~ Edgar Z. Friedenberg

Silence never won rights. They are not handed down from above; they are forced by pressures from below.

~ Roger Baldwin

A government operating in the shadow of secrecy stands in complete opposition to the society envisioned by the framers of our Constitution.

~ Damon Keith

Idleness is not doing nothing; *idleness is being free to do anything*.

~ Floyd Dell

Men imagine that a woman has no individual existence, and that she ought always to be absorbed in them.

~ George Sand

I believe September 11, 2001 projects a wake-up call to the world of collective consciousness. Each day I ask to learn the lesson, love more, and leave behind a legacy of peace.

~ Patricia Flor

The world is inescapably shot through with luck, because it is also shot through with freedom.

~ Joyce Cary

Many a one cannot loosen his own fetters, but is nevertheless his friend's emancipator.

~ Friedrich Nietzsche

Those who expect to reap the blessings of freedom must, like men, undergo the fatigues of supporting it.

~ Thomas Jefferson

A man must consider what a rich realm he abdicates when he becomes a conformist.

~ Ralph Waldo Emerson

It takes two to make peace.

~ John F. Kennedy

Censors are pretty sure to be fools.

~ James Harvey Robinson

Courage is the price that Life exacts for granting peace.

~ Amelia Earhart

We have gathered here to affirm a faith, a faith in a common purpose, a common conviction, a common devotion. Some of use have chosen America as the land of our adoption; the rest have come from those who did the same. For this reason we have some right to consider ourselves a picked group, a group of those who had the courage to break from the past and brave the dangers and the loneliness of a strange land. What was the object that nerved us, or those who went before us, to this choice? We sought liberty: freedom from oppression, freedom from want, freedom to be ourselves.

~ Learned Hand

No man can be fully free while his neighbor is not.

~ Richard Nixon

He who despises his own life is soon master of another's.

~ English proverb

I don't think anyone is free – one creates one's own prison.

~ Graham Sutherland

When a man is freed of religion, he has a better chance to live a normal and wholesome life.

~ Sigmund Freud

Men of war adapt about as readily to peace as men of peace adapt to war.

Property is the ultimate guarantor of freedom.

~ Walter Chambers

Heaven knows how to put a proper price on its goods; and it would be strange indeed if so celestial an article as freedom should not be highly rated.

~ Thomas Paine

Is life so dear, or peace so sweet, as to be purchased at the price of chains and slavery? Forbid it, almighty God! I know not what course others may take, but as for me, give me liberty, or give me death!

~ Patrick Henry (attributed)

One sword keeps another in the sheath.

~ George Herbert

When liberty destroys order, the hunger for order will destroy liberty.

~ Will Durant

The Constitution gives every American the inalienable right to make a damn fool of himself.

~ John Ciardi

Disappointments should be cremated, not embalmed.

~ Henry S. Haskins

There are more instances of the abridgement of the freedom of the people by gradual and silent encroachments of those in power than by violent and sudden usurpation.

~ James Madison

The right to be heard does not automatically include the right to be taken seriously.

~ Hubert Humphrey

We must guard against the acquisition of unwarranted influence...by the military-industrial complex. The potential for the disastrous rise of misplaced power exists and will persist.

~ Dwight D. Eisenhower

The liberty of the individual must be thus far limited; he must not make himself a nuisance to other people.

~ John Stuart Mill

It is a fair summary of history to say that the safeguards of liberty have frequently been forged in cases involving not very nice people.

~ Felix Frankfurter

I very much dislike the content, though not really the style, of 2 Live Crew's songs [the rap group from the early 90s who encountered stiff opposition from many Americans for their explicit lyrics and lewd content], but that is not the point. I don't have to go to their concert, or let my child listen to their albums. The problem for our American concept of liberty becomes when self-appointed moral agents attempt to decide, legislate and enforce unevenly what is "acceptable." Many wise people who have thought extensively on the philosophy of liberty would probably hold that no one should be the arbiter of what is "appropriate" and what is not. If you feel repulsed by the music 2 Live Crew makes, to allow it to be in the marketplace takes strength, but by adhering to strict ideals for freedom we can all rest more easily that someday Big Brother will not be determining that our perfectly reasonable choice is "inappropriate."

Peace is not an absence of war. It is a virtue, a state of mind, a disposition for benevolence, confidence, justice.

~ Benedict Spinoza

I would remind you that extremism in defense of justice is no vice.

~ Barry Goldwater

Outside, among your fellows, among strangers, you must preserve appearances, 100 things you cannot do; but inside, the terrible freedom!

~ Ralph Waldo Emerson

The spirit of liberty is the spirit which is not too sure that it is right.

~ Learned Hand

We can never be sure that the opinion we are endeavoring to stifle is a false opinion; and if we were sure, stifling it would be an evil still.

~ John Stuart Mill

Be peaceful, be courteous, obey the law, respect everyone, but if someone puts a hand on you, send him to the cemetery.

~ Malcolm X

Anxiety is the dizziness of freedom.

~ Soren Kierkegaard

Death is a softer thing by far than tyranny.

~ Aeschylus

The truth shall make you free.

~ John 8:32

There is hopeful symbolism in the fact that flags do not wave in a vacuum.

~ Arthur C. Clarke

I'm all in favor of keeping dangerous weapons out of the hands of fools. Let's start with typewriters.

~ Solomon Short

Either war is obsolete, or men are.

~ Buckminster Fuller

A man can be himself only so long as he is alone;.... If he does not love solitude, he will not love freedom; for it is only when he is alone that he is really free.

~ Arthur Schopenhauer

Censorship reflects society's lack of confidence in itself. It is a hallmark of an authoritarian regime.

~ Potter Stewart

Man did not enter into society to become worse than he was before, nor to have fewer rights than he had before, but to have those rights better secured.

~ Thomas Paine

Last year was the first time I had a Muslim student in my classroom. She rose and stood silently every morning as the rest of the class recited the Pledge of Allegiance. After September 11, 2001, she proudly announced one morning that her mother would now allow her to say the pledge with her classmates. In one small, third-grade classroom, we dealt a major blow to al-Qaeda.

~ Judy Johnson

I'm in favor of the government taking any measure it feels would make us more secure, with one condition: that it not upset our democracy's time-honored system of checks-and-balances, whereby the executive branch promotes it, the judiciary branch confirms its constitutionality, and the legislative branch is paid off to quietly kill it.

~ Dennis Miller

Anxiety is the dizziness of freedom.

~ Soren Kierkegaard

Big Brother is watching you.

~ George Orwell

The women of this nation, in 1876, have greater cause for discontent, rebellion, and revolution than the men of 1776.

~ Susan B. Anthony

Most people want security in this world, not liberty.

~ H. L. Mencken

What do you suppose will satisfy the soul, except to walk free and own no superior?

~ Walt Whitman

They have rights who dare to maintain them.

~ James Russell Lowell

Few rich men own their own property; the property owns them.

~ Robert Ingersoll

To give up the task of reforming society is to give up one's responsibility as a free man.

~ Alan Paton

We are willing enough to praise freedom when she is safely tucked away in the past and cannot be a nuisance. In the present, amidst dangers whose outcome we cannot foresee, we get nervous about her, and admit censorship.

~ E. M. Forster

It is easier to lead men to combat, stirring up their passions, than to restrain them and direct them toward the patient labors of peace.

~ Andre Gide

It is a besetting vice of democracies to substitute public opinion for law.   This is the usual form in which masses of men exhibit their tyranny.

~ James Fennimore Cooper

Do not value money for any more nor any less than it is worth; it is a good servant but a bad master.

~ Alexandre Dumas

They must know but little of mankind who imagine that, having once been seduced by luxury, they can ever renounce it.

~ Jean Jacques Rousseau

To be truly free, it takes more determination, courage, introspection and restraint than to be in shackles.

~ Pietro Bellusch

Democracy...is a society in which the unbeliever feels undisturbed and at home. If there were only half a dozen unbelievers in America, their well-being would be a test of our democracy.

~ Alfred North Whitehead

You may fetter my leg, but Zeus himself cannot get the better of my free will.

~ Epictetus

Men fight for liberty and win it with hard knocks. Their children, brought up easy, let it slip away again, poor fools. And their grandchildren are once again slaves.

~ D. H. Lawrence

Let every nation know, whether it wishes us well or ill, that we shall pay any price, bear any burden, meet any hardship, support any friend, oppose any foe to assure the survival and the success of liberty.... My fellow citizens of the world: ask not what America will do for you, but what together we can do for the freedom of man.

~ John F. Kennedy

No man is bound by any obligation unless it has first been freely accepted.

~ Ugo Betti

Freedom is the will to be responsible to ourselves.

~ Friedrich Nietzsche

The despotism of custom is everywhere the standing hindrance to human advancement.

~ John Stuart Mill

When people are free to do as they please, they usually imitate each other.

~ Eric Hoffer

Wherever you have an efficient government you have a dictatorship.

~ Harry S. Truman

None can love freedom heartily, but good men – the rest love not freedom, but license.

~ John Milton

You may give children your love but not your thoughts, for they have their own thoughts.

~ Kahlil Gibran

There is no easy road to freedom.

~ Nelson Mandela

If you want to find a politician free of any influence, you can find Adolf Hitler, who made up his own mind.

~ Eugene McCarthy

You can choose a ready guide in some celestial voice.
If you choose not to decide, you still haven't made a choice.
You can choose from phantom fears and kindness that can kill;
I will choose a path that's clear, I will choose freewill.

~ Neil Peart

In the world at large an increasing inclination to stretch unduly the powers of society over the individual, both by force of opinion and even by that of legislation.

~ John Stuart Mill

When you have robbed a man of everything, he is no longer in your power. He is free again.

~ Aleksandr Solzhenitsyn

You can no more win a war than you can win an earthquake.

~ Jeannette Rankin

Liberty means responsibility. That is why most men dread it.

~ George Bernard Shaw

When the white man governs himself, that is self-government; but when he governs himself and another man, that is more than self-government – that is despotism.

~ Abraham Lincoln

Strong government, to some extent, is in response to huge problems.

~ John Kenneth Galbraith

Censorship that comes from the outside assumes about people an inability to make reasoned choices.

~ George Carlin

For it isn't enough to talk about peace. One must believe in it. And it isn't enough to believe in it. One must work at it.

~ Eleanor Roosevelt

If mankind minus one were of one opinion, then mankind is no more justified in silencing the one than the one - if he had the power - would be justified in silencing mankind.

~ John Stuart Mill

You cannot simultaneously prevent and prepare for war.

~ Albert Einstein

With all the mass media concentrated in a few hands, the ancient faith in the competition of ideas in the free market seems like a hollow echo of a much simpler day.

~ Kingman Brewster, Jr.

Democracy is a device that ensures we shall be governed no better than we deserve.

~ George Bernard Shaw

Trying to be a first-rate reporter on the average American newspaper is like trying to play Bach's 'St. Matthew's Passion' on a ukulele.

~ Bagdikian's Observation

A religion old or new, that stressed the magnificence of the universe as revealed by modern science, might be able to draw forth reserves of reverence and awe hardly tapped by the conventional faiths. Sooner or later such a religion will emerge.

~ Carl Sagan

I know not with what weapons World War III will be fought, but World War IV will be fought with sticks and stones.

~ Albert Einstein

Until you've lost your reputation, you never realize what a burden it was.

~ Margaret Mitchell

God, as representing objective values, is our master. If, however, God is dead, the effect is exhilarating ...*our sea lies open again*...

~ Friedrich Nietzsche

Man is free at the moment he wishes to be.

~ Voltaire

A child becomes an adult when he realizes that he has a right not only to be right but also to be wrong.

~ Thomas Szasz

So far war has been the only force that can discipline a whole community, and until an equivalent discipline is organized, I believe that war must have its way.

~ William James

People demand freedom of speech to make up for the freedom of thought which they avoid.

~ Soren Kierkegaard

The only thing that saves us from the bureaucracy is inefficiency. An efficient bureaucracy is the greatest threat to liberty.

~ Eugene McCarthy

The whole history of the progress of human liberty shows that all concessions yet made to her august claims have been born of earnest struggle.... If there is no struggle, there is no progress. Those who profess to favor freedom, and yet deprecate agitation, are men who want crops without thunder and lightening. They want the ocean without the awful roar of its many waters.

~ Frederick Douglass

Once freedom lights its beacon in a man's heart, the gods are powerless against him.

~ Jean-Paul Sartre

I disapprove of what you say, but I will defend to the death your right to say it.

~ Voltaire

We who lived in concentration camps can remember the men who walked through the huts comforting others, giving away their last piece of bread. They may have been few in numbers, but offer sufficient proof that everything can be taken from a man but one thing: the last of the human freedoms to [determine one's] attitude in any given set of circumstances – to choose one's own way.

~Viktor Frankl

Is not the stifling of opinion worse than any single opinion, no matter how subversive?

MODESTY, RESPECT & TOLERANCE

Happiness is a butterfly, which, when pursued, is always just beyond your grasp, but which, if you will sit down quietly, may alight upon you.

~ Nathaniel Hawthorne

Violence attempts to constrain the other's freedom, to force him to act in the way we desire, but with ultimate lack of concern, with indifference to the other's own existence or destiny.

~ R. D. Laing

Understanding a person does not mean condoning; it only means that one does not accuse him as if one were God or a judge placed above him.

~ Erich Fromm

Human beings are perhaps never more frightening than when they are convinced beyond doubt that they are right.

~ Laurens Van Der Post

Men never do evil so cheerfully and so completely as when they do so from religious conviction.

~ Blaise Pascal

You can tell the character of every man when you see how he receives praise.

~ Lucius Annaeus Seneca

The true way to be deceived is to think oneself more clever than others.

~ Francois, Duc de La Rochefoucauld

A difference of opinion is what makes horse races and missionaries.

~ Will Rogers

In the end, I'm never satisfied that I have a complete understanding of any problem.

~ Michael E. Kerr

It astounds us to come upon other egotists, as though we alone had the right to be selfish and full of eagerness to live.

~ Jules Renard

Take egotism out and you would castrate the benefactor.

~ Ralph Waldo Emerson

The modern world belongs to the half-educated, a rather difficult class, because they do not realize how little they know.

~ William R. Inge

More and more I use the quickness of my mind to pick the mind of other people and use their knowledge as my own.

~ Eleanor Roosevelt

Jesse Jackson is a man of the cloth. Cashmere.

~ Mort Sahl

We believe nothing so firmly as what we least know.

~ Michel de Montaigne

Observe due measure, for right timing is in all things the most important factor.

~ Hesiod

What's done to children, they will do to society.

~ Karl Menninger

The morning of September 11, 2001, my nation awoke under siege. Suddenly, my neighbors' unknown faces became apparent to me: our tears had the same taste and reflected the same color; their sadness was my sadness. Even those gods to whom we all started praying, for a moment, became one.

~ Lorenzo Rodriguez

To be uncertain is to be uncomfortable, but to be certain is ridiculous.

~ Chinese proverb

Don't judge anyone harshly until you have been through his experiences.

~ Johann Wolfgang von Goethe

The greater a man is, the more distasteful is praise and flattery to him.

~ John Burroughs

Modesty is the gentle art of enhancing your charm by pretending not to be aware of it.

~ Oliver Herford

The first thing to learn in intercourse with others is noninterference with their own peculiar ways of being happy, provided those ways do not assume to interfere by violence with ours.

~ William James

The opposite of talking isn't listening. The opposite of talking is waiting.

~ Fran Leibowitz

True intelligence very readily conceives of an intelligence superior to its own; and this is why truly intelligent men are modest.

~ Andre Gide

The trite objects of human efforts – possessions, outward success, luxury – have always seemed to me contemptible.

~ Albert Einstein

To judge a man's character by only one of its manifestations is like judging the sea by a jugful of its water.

~ Paul Eldridge

We always admire the other fellow more after we have tried to do his job.

~ William C. Feather

Ambition is the grand enemy of all peace.

~ John Cowper Powys

Pocket all your knowledge with your watch and never pull it out in company unless desired.

~ Lord Chesterfield

A man's ruin lies in his tongue.

~ Egyptian proverb

Be nice to people on your way up because you might meet them on your way down.

~ Jimmy Durante

After listening to thousands of pleas for pardon to offenders, I can hardly recall a case where I did not feel that I might have fallen as my fellow man had done, if I had been subjected to the same demoralizing influences and pressed by the same temptations.

~ Horatio Seymour

The true spirit of conversation consists more in bringing out the cleverness of others than in showing a great deal of it yourself.

~ Jean de la Bruyere

Nature has given to men one tongue, but two ears, that we may hear from others twice as much as we speak.

~ Epictetus

When a man is wrapped up in himself he makes a pretty small package.

~ John Ruskin

If I have seen farther it is by standing on the shoulders of giants.

~ Isaac Newton

The mystery of the beginning of all things is insoluble by us; and I for one must be content to remain agnostic.

~ Charles Darwin

From fanaticism to barbarism is only one step.

~ Denis Diderot

Never try to reasons the prejudice out of a man. It was not reasoned into him, and cannot be reasoned out.

~ Sydney Smith

In all affairs, love, religion, politics, or business, it's a healthy idea, now and then, to hang a question mark on things you have long taken for granted.

~ Bertrand Russell

Just because your voice reaches halfway around the world doesn't mean you are wiser than when it reached only to the end of the bar.

~ Edward R. Murrow

The dinosaur's eloquent lesson is that is some bigness is good, an overabundance of bigness is not necessarily better.

~ Eric Johnston

Patience and passage of time do more than strength and fury.

~ Jean de la Fontaine

If you want people to think well of you, do not speak well of yourself.

~ Blaise Pascal

When the man is at home, his standing in society is well known and quietly taken; but when he is abroad, it is problematic, and is dependent on the success of his manners.

~ Ralph Waldo Emerson

It's perfectly understandable to discover the roots of your religion and want to share it with everyone you meet. By the same token, please understand the basic tenets of my religion, which specifically proscribe that: should you knock on my door, corner me on an elevator, or sit next to me on a flight yammering on and on about how your way is the right way, I am morally obligated by the elders of my church to tell you to shut the fuck up.

~ Dennis Miller

Modesty is the only bait when you angle for praise.

~ Lord Chesterfield

Short of genius, a rich man cannot imagine poverty.

~ Charles Peguy

To be clever enough to get all that money, one must be stupid enough to want it.

~ G. K. Chesterton

Don't ever take a fence down until you know why it was put up.

~ Robert Frost

In a war of ideas it is people who get killed.

~ Stanislaw J. Lec

He who wants a rose must respect the thorn.

~ Persian proverb

This is the devilish thing about foreign affairs: they are foreign and will not always conform to our whim.

~ James Reston

There is nothing noble about being superior to some other person. True nobility is in being superior to your previous self.

~ Hindustani proverb

No man can put a chain about the ankle of his fellow man without at last finding the other end fastened around his own neck.

~ Frederick Douglass

Where there are no tigers, a wildcat is very self-important.

~ Korean proverb

If each of us goes to the Holy Book, I don't think we'll ever reach a solution.

~ Prince Saud al-Faisal

The peak of tolerance is most readily achieved by those who are not burdened with convictions.

~ Alexander Chase

The equal toleration of all religions...is the same thing as atheism.

~ Pope Leo XIII

Mediocrity knows nothing higher than itself, but talent instantly recognizes genius.

~ Arthur Conan Doyle

Everyone is a prisoner of his own experiences. No one can eliminate prejudices – just recognize them.

~ Edward R. Murrow

Admiration for ourselves and our institutions is too often measured by our contempt and dislike for foreigners.

~ William Ralph Inge

Success has ruined many a man.

~ Benjamin Franklin

It is always the secure who are humble.

~ G. K. Chesterton

It is the nature of desire not to be satisfied, and most men live only for the gratification of it. The beginning of reform is not so much to equalize property as to train the noble sort of natures not to desire more, and to prevent the lower from getting more.

~ Aristotle

I like the moment when I break a man's ego.

~ Bobby Fischer

When a man speaks of his strength, he whispers his weakness.

~ John M. Shanahan

It is absurd and disgraceful to live magnificently and luxuriously when so many are hungry.

~ Clement of Alexandria

To all of you out there who don't cover your mouth, who don't have the money ready when you get to the toll booth, who do burp so loudly in public that others wonder where the epicenter was, to all of you dwelling out there on the crassy knoll -- if you don't want to come and join the rest of us in this noble pursuit of good manners, we all cordially invite you to please, go fuck yourself!

~ Dennis Miller

We have just enough religion to make us hate, but not enough to make us love one another.

~ Jonathan Swift

Without feelings of respect, what is there to distinguish men from beasts?

~ Confucius

The unbelievers shall have garments of fire fitted to them; boiling water shall be poured on their heads; their bowels shall be dissolved thereby, and also their skins, and they shall be beaten with maces of iron.

~ The Koran

Praise shames me, for I secretly beg for it.

~ Rabindranath Tagore

There's no one so transparent as the person who thinks he's deep.

~ Somerset Maugham

Do not make yourself so big. You're not so small.

~ Jewish proverb

Luxury... corrupts at once rich and poor, the rich by possession and the poor by covetousness.

~ Jean Jacques Rousseau

There is a law that man should love his neighbor as himself. In a few hundred years it should be as natural to mankind as breathing or the upright gait; but if he does not learn it he must perish.

~ Alfred Adler

The urge to cheat, steal and kill is a holdover from a time when we lived by the anything-goes Darwinian law of survival. Remember, it's only since 1972 that we started telling each other to have a nice day.

~ Dennis Miller

True patriotism doesn't exclude an understanding of the patriotism of others.

~ Queen Elizabeth II

Even in a palace it is possible to live well.

~ Marcus Aurelius

Mediocre minds usually dismiss anything which reaches beyond their own understanding.

~ Francois, Duc de La Rochefoucauld

To be simple is the best thing in the world; to be modest is the next best thing. I am not sure about being quiet.

~ G. K. Chesterton

Facism... throws the noxious theories of so-called liberalism on the rubbish heap.

~ Benito Mussolini

Nothing so dates a man as to decry the younger generation.

~ Adlai Stevenson

It is well, when judging a friend, to remember that he is judging you with the same godlike and superior impartiality.

~ Arnold Bennett

Examinations are formidable even to the best prepared, for the greatest fool may ask more than the wisest man can answer.

~ Charles Caleb Colton

Some people take more care to hide their wisdom than their folly.

~ Jonathan Swift

The world is made up for the most part of morons and natural tyrants, sure of themselves, strong in their own opinions, never doubting anything.

~ Clarence Darrow

Never express yourself more clearly than you are able to think.

~ Niels Bohr

Human beings are perhaps never more frightening than when they are convinced beyond doubt that they are right.

~ Joseph Addison

Respect for the fragility and importance of an individual life is still the mark of an educated man.

~ Norman Cousins

Quarrels would not last long if the fault were only on one side.

~ Francois, Duc de La Rochefoucauld

Life is a long lesson in humility.

~ James M. Barrie

Modesty is an overrated virtue.

~ John Kenneth Galbraith

Take counsel with the ignorant as well as the wise, for the limits of proficiency cannot be reached and no person is ever fully skilled.

~ Egyptian Magistrate Ptah-Hotep

Don't use a big word where a diminutive one will suffice.

~ Unknown

The surest way to knock the chip off a fellow's shoulder is by patting him on the back.

~ Zig Ziglar

Correction does much, but encouragement does more. Encouragement after censure is as the sun after a shower.

~ Johann Wolfgang von Goethe

No man ever listened himself out of a job.

~ Calvin Coolidge

Most conversations are simply monologues delivered in the presence of witnesses.

~ Margaret Millar

Children are as respectable as adults.

Honest disagreement is often a good sign of progress.

~ Mohandas K. Gandhi

The trouble with the world is that the stupid are cocksure and the intelligent are full of doubt.

~ Bertrand Russell

In literature as in love, we are astonished at what is chosen by others.

~ Andre Maurois

If your spouse does not find your teasing, hostile, or sarcastic jokes funny, beware: that is and act of belligerence, not humor.

~ John Gottman

A good listener is usually thinking about something else.

~ Kin Hubbard

We hate some people because we do not know them; and will not know them because we hate them.

~ Charles Caleb Colton

Hesitance is as true as dogmatism.

Is it good to have friends whom you don't agree with? Temporarily. But it has always been my purpose to get them to change their minds.

~ John Kenneth Galbraith

Nothing has an uglier look to us than reason, when it is not on our side.

~ George Savile

It is only a fool who never suspects he could be foolishly mistaken.

~ Michel de Montaigne

The denunciation of the young is a necessary part of the hygiene of older people, and greatly assists in the circulation of the blood

~ Logan Pearsall Smith

There is no human problem which could not be solved if people would simply do as I advise.

~ Gore Vidal

I can't complain, but sometimes I still do.

~ Joe Walsh

Intolerance is natural and logical, for in every dissenting opinion lies an assumption of superior wisdom.

~ Ambrose Bierce

If you're trying to show off for other people, forget it. They will look down on you anyhow. And if you're trying to show off for people at the bottom, forget it. They will only envy you. Status will get you nowhere.

~ Morrie Schwartz

I know that there are people who do not love their fellow man, and I hate people like that!

~ Tom Lehrer

Few things are harder to put up with than the annoyance of a good example.

~ Mark Twain

Fortune does not change men, it unmasks them.

~Suzanne Necker

As emperor, Rome is my homeland; but as a man, I am a citizen of the world.

~ Marcus Aurelius

Millions of innocent men, women and children, since the introduction of Christianity, have been burnt, tortured, fined and imprisoned; yet we have not advanced one inch towards uniformity.

~ Thomas Jefferson

When one attends to another's garden, one's own garden tends to sprout weeds.

Do not condemn the judgment of another because it differs from your own. You may both be wrong.

~ Dandemis

Be not angry that you cannot make others as you wish them to be, since you cannot make yourself as you wish to be.

~ Thomas a Kempis

Wait for the wisest of all counselors, Time.

~ Pericles

MAGNANIMITY & ALTRUISM

One thing I know: the only ones among you who will be really happy are those who will have sought and found how to serve.

~ Albert Schweitzer

On the whole, human beings want to be good, but not too good, and not quite all the time.

~ George Orwell

Why were we able to put hundreds of thousands of troops and support personnel in Saudi Arabia within a few months to fight Saddam Hussein when we are unable to mobilize hundreds of teachers or doctors and nurses and social workers for desperately underserved inner cities and rural areas to fight the tyranny of poverty and ignorance and child neglect and abuse?

~ Marian Wright Edelman

I now perceive on immense omission in my psychology — the deepest principle of human nature is the craving to be appreciated.

~ William James

Leave off wishing to deserve any thanks from anyone, thinking that anyone can ever become grateful.

~ Galius Valerius Catullus

Always forgive your enemies; nothing annoys them so much.

~ Oscar Wilde

Teachers, who educate children, deserve more honor than parents, who merely gave them birth; for the latter provided mere life, while the former ensure a good life.

~ Aristotle

The greatest spirits are capable of the greatest vices as well as the greatest virtues.

~ Rene Descartes

There's nothing wrong with high taxes on high income.

~ George Carlin

Whether learning has made more proud men or good men may be a question.

~ Anonymous

Comfort the afflicted and afflict the comfortable.

~ Finley Peter Dunne

Violence is as American as cherry pie.

~ H. Rap Brown

Every man is guilty of all the good he didn't do.

~ Voltaire

One can pay back the gift of gold, but one dies forever in debt to those who are kind.

~ Malayan proverb

No man deserves to be praised for his goodness unless he has the strength of character to be wicked. All other goodness is generally nothing but indolence or impotence of will.

~ Francois, Duc de La Rochefoucauld

Out of the experience of an extraordinary human disaster that lasted too long must be born a society of which humanity will be proud.

~ Nelson Mandela

The legacy of a man is created through a few remarkable situations.
What honor lies in philosophizing from one's soporific armchair?
'Tis a world full of pessimists, of mutable morals~
Indeed, those who show greatness are becoming increasingly rare.

From the ashes of destruction, I hope the outpouring of kindness and commitment that arose after 9/11/2001 continues. There could be no better monument than increasing our positive intentions and actions toward our fellow human beings. This has the power to change the world. Let the difference begin with us.

~ Cathryn Golden

When love became devotion instead of possession, marriage reached the climax of its slow ascent from brutality.

~ Will Durant

I expect to pass through this world but once. Any good therefore that I can do, or any kindness or abilities that I can show to any fellow creature, let me do it now. Let me not defer or neglect it, for I shall not pass this way again.

~ William Penn

He who waits to do a great deal of good at once, will never do anything.

~ Samuel Johnson

Man is the missing link between the ape and the human being.

~ Anonymous

Mistrust your zeal for doing good to others.

~ Abbe Huvelin

The best practical advice I can give to the present generation is to practice the virtue which the Christians call love.

~ Bertrand Russell

The purpose of life is not to be happy – but to *matter*, to be productive, to be useful, to have it make some difference that you have lived at all.

~ Leo Rosten

Great men are always linked to their age by some weakness or other.

~ Johann Wolfgang von Goethe

Man uses his intelligence less in the care of his own species than he does in his care of anything else he owns or governs.

~ Abraham Meyerson

Blessed are those who can give without remembering, and take without forgetting.

~ Elizabeth Bibesco

The world knows nothing of its greatest men.

~ Henry Taylor

He has the right to criticize who has the heart to help.

~ Abraham Lincoln

Some people strengthen society just by being the kind of people they are.

~ John W. Gardner

The reformative effect of punishment is a belief that dies hard, chiefly because it is so satisfying to our sadistic impulses.

~ Bertrand Russell

I believe that man will not merely endure; he will prevail. He is immortal, not because he alone among creatures has an inexhaustible voice, but because he has a soul, a spirit capable of compassion and sacrifice and endurance.

~ William Faulkner

Compassion is not weakness, and concern for the unfortunate is not socialism.

~ Hubert H. Humphrey

I was born into it and there was nothing I could do about it. It was there, like air or food, or any other element. The only question with wealth is what you do with it.

~ John D. Rockefeller, Jr.

Whatever you are, be a good one.

~ Abraham Lincoln

The value of a man should be seen in what he gives and not what he is able to receive.

~ Albert Einstein

Non-violence is a powerful and just weapon. It is a weapon unique in history, which cuts without wounding and ennobles the man who wields it. It is a sword that heals.

~ Martin Luther King, Jr.

We can have democracy in this country or we can have great wealth concentrated in the hands of a few, but we can't have both.

~ Louis D. Brandeis

Real maturity is to imagine the humanity of every person as fully as you believe in your own humanity.

~ Tobias Wolff

Making money is fun, but it's pointless if you don't use the power it brings.

~ John Bentley

There's only one corner of the universe you can be certain of improving and that's your own self.

~ Aldous Huxley

In the case of political, and even religious, leaders it is often very doubtful whether they have done more harm or good.

~ Albert Einstein

I consider myself a Hindu, Christian, Moslem, Jew, Buddhist, and Confucian.

~ Mohandas K. Gandhi

If the world were merely seductive, that would be easy. If it were merely challenging, that would be no problem. But I rise in the morning torn between a desire to improve (or save) the world and a desire to enjoy (or savor) the world. This makes it hard to plan the day.

~ E. B. White

One of the signs of passing youth is the birth of a sense of fellowship with other human beings as we take our place among them.

~ Virginia Woolfe

Where love rules, there is no will to power; and where power predominates, love is lacking. The one is the shadow of the other.

~ Carl Jung

The true meaning of life is to plant trees, under whose shade you do not expect to sit.

~ Nelson Henderson

Who takes the child by the hand takes the mother by the heart.

~ German proverb

Regarding liberal concern for the world's disfranchised, I think that on a small scale it is helpful – if not altruistic. However, regarding guilt about not being able to help everyone, do everything, and change the way the system works, I would say this: be part of the solution and not part of the problem and you can feel good enough (though not great). You and I are not the originator of luck. We are not the designer of the universe, nor do we have the power to manipulate complex sociological phenomena with a simple benevolent thought. Live consciously and hope that the darker side of human nature does not ruin this experiment that's been running for the last 20,000 years.

Giving is the highest expression of potency.

~ Erich Fromm

The most certain test by which we judge whether a country is really free is the amount of security enjoyed by minorities.

~ John, Lord Acton

It is a dangerous thing to reform anyone.

~ Oscar Wilde

Charity is injurious unless it helps the recipient to become independent of it.

~ John D. Rockefeller

The greatest pleasure I know is to do a good action by stealth, and to have it found out by accident.

~ Charles Lamb

The meaning of good and bad, or better and worse, is simply helping or hurting.

~ Ralph Waldo Emerson

The problem of our age is the proper administration of wealth, so that the ties of brotherhood may still bind together the rich and poor in harmonious relationship.

~ Andrew Carnegie

I feel bad that I don't feel worse.

~ Michael Frayn

Pity may represent little more than the impersonal concern which prompts the mailing of a check, but true sympathy is the personal concern which demands the giving of one's soul.

~ Martin Luther King, Jr.

Children need love, especially when they do not deserve it.

~ Harold S. Hulbert

People of privilege will always risk their complete destruction rather than surrender any material part of their advantage.

~ John Kenneth Galbraith

The human race has improved everything except the human race.

~ Adlai Stevenson

God waits to win back his own flowers as gifts from man's hands.

~ Rabindranath Tagore

A great ship asks deep water.

~ George Herbert

You cannot do a kindness too soon, for you never know how soon it will be too late.

~ Ralph Waldo Emerson

Social progress means a checking of the [evolutionary] process at every step and substituting for it...the ethical process, which is not the survival of those who happen to be the fittest...but of those who are ethically the best.

~ T. H. Huxley

The superior man...does not set his mind either for or against anything; he will pursue whatever is right.... The superior man thinks of virtue, the common man of comfort.

~ Confucius

I am opposed to socialism because it dreams ingeniously of good, truth, beauty, and equal rights.

~ Friedrich Nietzsche

He is rich who hath enough to be charitable.

~ Sir Thomas Browne

The small share of happiness attainable by man exists only insofar as he is able to cease to think of himself.

~ Theodor Reik

We must embark on a bold new program for making the benefit of our scientific and industrial progress available for the improvement and growth of underdeveloped areas.

~ Harry S. Truman

The world will never be ready for its saints.

~ George Bernard Shaw

The only reward of virtue is virtue; the only way to have a friend is to be one.

~ Ralph Waldo Emerson

One never dives into the water to save a drowning man more eagerly than when there are others present who dare not take the risk.

~ Friedrich Nietzsche

There are a thousand hacking at the branches of evil to one who is striking at the root.

~ Henry David Thoreau

The test of our progress is not whether we add more to the abundance of those who have much; it is whether we provide enough for those who have too little.

~ Franklin D. Roosevelt

Blood cannot be washed out with blood.

~ Persian proverb

We have the means of removing starvation and disease.... One thing is lacking: good will and understanding.

~ Vannevar Bush

To be a philosopher is not merely to have subtle thoughts, nor even to found a school, but to love wisdom so as to live according to its dictates, a life of simplicity, independence, magnanimity, and trust.

~ Henry David Thoreau

The prudent man does himself good; the virtuous man does good to others.

~ Voltaire

If thou wouldst be perfect, go and sell that thou hast, and give to the poor, and thou shalt have treasure in heaven.

~ Matthew 19:21

We pardon to the extent that we love.

~ Francois, Duc de La Rochefoucauld

I know of no country...where the love of money has taken a stronger hold on the affections of men and where a profounder contempt is expressed for the theory of the permanent equality of property.

~ Alexis de Tocqueville

You are forgiven for your happiness and your successes only if you generously consent to share them.

~ Albert Camus

Most of us are at some time or other impelled...to take a hand in solving the problems of society, and most of us know in our hearts that it is our business to leave the world a little better than we found it.

~ Cyril Joad

We come nearest to the great when we are great in humility.

~ Rabindranath Tagore

A mark of maturity seems to be the range and extent of one's feeling of self-involvement in abstract ideals.

~ Gordon Allport

Charms strike the sight, but merit wins the soul.

~ Alexander Pope

You need more tact in the dangerous art of giving than in any other social action.

~ William Bolitho

The man who dies rich dies disgraced.

~ Andrew Carnegie

Goodness is the only investment that never fails.

~ Henry David Thoreau

Rarely do great beauty and great virtue dwell together.

~ Petrarch

Humanitarianism is a manifestation of stupidity and cowardice.

~ Adolf Hitler

It is true that armor can feel cumbersome;
The weight of duty does encumber the good.
He or she who is heroic strives to *become;*
Our hearts drive us to do as we know we should.

We would frequently be ashamed of our good deeds if people saw all he motives that produced them.

~ Francois, Duc de La Rochefoucauld

Magnanimity will not consider the prudence of its motives.

~ Luc de Clapiers de Vauvenargues

As we accept our children, we free them to be who they are in a world that is trying to tell them every day to be someone else.

~ Tim Hansel

Minds are not conquered by arms, but by love and magnanimity.

~ Baruch Spinoza

A man makes no noise over a good deed, but passes on to another.

~ Marcus Aurelius

Too many have dispensed with generosity in order to practice charity.

~ Albert Camus

To the world you may be one person, but to one person, you may be the world.

~ Unknown

America may be unique in being a country which has leapt from barbarism to decadence without touching civilization.

~ John O'Hara

Our deeds determine us, as much as we determine our deeds.

~ George Eliot

Of cheerfulness or a good temper – the more it is spent, the more of it remains.

~ Ralph Waldo Emerson

In richer countries, such as ours, I want to see everybody assured of a basic income.

~ John Kenneth Galbraith

The truest mark of a human matured to their potential
Is the exercise of mercy; it's absolutely essential.
The exalted position of Popes and thrones of monarchs
Affords the hypocrites the opportunity to prey like sharks.

Be ashamed to die until you have won some victory for humanity

~ Horace Mann

Liberals feel unworthy of their possessions. Conservatives feel they deserve everything they've stolen.

~ Mort Sahl

Great spirits exemplify numerous virtues.
They view the world in vibrant hues.
She personifies the loftiest human values.
He knows many elusive and profound truths.

The best time to plant a tree is 20 years ago. The second best time is now.

~Chinese proverb

Believe, when you are most unhappy, that there is something for you to do in the world. So long as you can sweeten another's pain, life is not in vain.

~ Helen Keller

Keep me away from the wisdom which does not weep, the philosophy which does not laugh, and the greatness which does not bow before children.

~ Kahlil Gibran

We need to try to save the Earth at least as fast as it's being destroyed

~ David Brower

The greatest use of life is to spend it for something that will outlast it.

~ William James

When a man tells you that he got rich through hard work, ask him: 'Whose?'

~ Don Marquis

Attention is an act of will, of work against the inertia of our own minds.

~ M. Scott Peck

So soon as prudence has begun to grow up in the brain, like a dismal fungus, it finds its first expression in a paralysis of generous acts.

~ Robert Louis Stevenson

The time is always right to do what's right.

~ Martin Luther King, Jr.

A teacher affects eternity; he can never tell where his influence stops

~ Henry Adams

More and more I have come to value charity and love of one's fellow being above all else.

~ Albert Einstein

The wicked are always surprised to find that the good can be clever.

~ Luc de Clapiers de Vauvenargues

The evil that is in this world almost always comes of ignorance, and good intentions may do as much harm as malevolence if they lack understanding.

~ Albert Camus

On the heights, it is warmer than those in the valley imagine.

~ Friedrich Nietzsche

Goodness without wisdom always accomplishes evil.

~ Robert A. Heinlein

Men of ill judgment oft ignore the good that lies within their hands, till they have lost it.

~ Sophocles

It is a very delicate job to forgive a man, without lowering him in his estimation, and yours too.

~ Josh Billings

Poverty does not produce unhappiness; it produces degradation.

~ George Bernard Shaw

HONOR, INTEGRITY & MORALITY

If you pick up a starving dog and make him prosperous, he will not bite you. This is the principal difference between a dog and a man.

~ Mark Twain

There are three classes of men - lovers of wisdom, lovers of honor, and lovers of gain.

~ Plato

When a man says he approves of something in principle, it means he hasn't the slightest intention of putting it into practice.

~ Otto von Bismarck

The moral constitution of any society determines the number of voluntary deaths.

~ Emile Durkheim

Many a crown shines spotless now that yet was deeply sullied in he winning.

~ Johann von Schiller

What other dungeon is so dark as one's own heart! What jailer so inexorable as one's self!

~ Nathaniel Hawthorne

You heard of honest Socrates
The man who never lied:
They weren't so grateful as you'd think
Instead the rulers fixed to have him tried
And handed him the poisoned drink.
How honest was the people's noble son.
The world however did not wait
But soon observed what followed on.
It's honesty that brought him to that state.
How fortunate the man with none....

~ Bertolt Brecht

My father was never particularly interested in making money. And neither am I. He always said that if you do the right thing, and build your bridges strong, it will come automatically.

~ Philip K. Wrigley

Men err when they think they can be inhuman exploiters in their business life, and loving husbands and fathers at home.

~ Smiley Blanton

Our distrust is very expensive.

~ Ralph Waldo Emerson

I should say sincerity, a deep, great, genuine sincerity, is that characteristic of all men in any way heroic.

~ Thomas Carlyle

Principles always become a matter of vehement discussion when practice is at an ebb.

~ George Gissing

A smile is the chosen vehicle for all ambiguities.

~ Herman Melville

Oh, what a tangled web we weave,
When first we practice to deceive!

~ Walter Scott

Being conservative with our social interventions ~ even though they cost money ~ is not just an ideology or attitudinal preference, it is a moral choice.

Whenever there is lost the consciousness that every man is an object of concern for us just because he is a man, civilization and morals are shaken, and the advance to fully developed inhumanity is only a question of time.

~ Albert Schweitzer

The ring passed to Isildur, who had this one chance to destroy evil forever. But, the hearts of men are easily corrupted.

~ J.R.R. Tolkien

Evil deeds do not prosper; the slow man catches up with the swift.

~ Homer

His lack of education is more than compensated for by his keenly developed moral bankruptcy.

~ Woody Allen

The man who acts never has any conscience; no one has any conscience but the man who thinks.

~ Johann Wolfgang von Goethe

The universe seems bankrupt as soon as we begin to discuss the characters of individuals.

~ Henry David Thoreau

I hope I shall always possess firmness and virtue enough to maintain what I consider the most enviable of all titles, the character of an honest man.

~ George Washington

Morality is contraband in war.

~ Mohandas K. Gandhi

There may come a time in every human's life where they must instantly choose between two monumental paths. One must act strongly and bravely, for the cost of one is but death, whereas the penalty for the other is a lifetime of shame.

When men grow virtuous in old age, they only make a sacrifice to God of the devil's leavings.

~ Jonathan Swift

There is no greater delight than to be conscious of sincerity on self-examination.

~ Mencius

I think Dostoevsky was right, that every human being must have a point at which he stands against the culture, where he says, 'This is me and the damned world can go to hell.'

~ Rollo May

Integrity simply means a willingness not to violate one's identity.

~ Erich Fromm

With every physical pain, my moral fiber unravels a little.

~ Mason Cooley

Never let your sense of morals get in the way of doing what's right.

~ Isaac Asimov

What is morality in any given time or place? It is what the majority then and there happen to like, and immorality is what they dislike.

~ Alfred North Whitehead

True patriotism hates injustice in its own land more than anywhere else.

~ Clarence Darrow

There's right and wrong. Do one and you're living. Do the other and you may be walking around, but you're as dead as a beaver hat.

~ Davy Crockett

It is customary these days to ignore what should be done in favor of what pleases us.

~ Plautus

If a man thinks about his physical or moral state, he usually discovers that he is ill.

~ Johann Wolfgang von Goethe

We've all seen the man at the liquor store begging for your change,
The hair on his face is dirty, dreadlocked and full of mange.
He asks a man for what he could spare with shame in his eyes,
"Get a job, you fucking slob" is all he replies.
God forbid you ever had to walk a mile in his shoes,
'Cause then you really might know what it's like to sing the blues.

~ Erik Schrody

All reform except a moral one will prove unavailing.

~ Thomas Carlyle

Neither man nor angel can discern hypocrisy, the only evil that walks invisible.

~ John Milton

There are millions of people out there who at this very moment are uttering "love this" and "love that" and "I love you," and they have no concept of what that really means.

~ Dustin Beall

Dignity does not consist of possessing honors, but in deserving them.

~ Aristotle

A man has honor if he holds himself to an ideal of conduct though it is inconvenient, unprofitable or dangerous to do so.

~ Walter Lippmann

We are in bondage to the law in order that we may be free.

~ Marcus Tullius Cicero

Being a hero is about the shortest-lived profession on earth.

~ Will Rogers

If a man hasn't discovered something that he will die for, he isn't fit to live.

~ Martin Luther King

The good should be grateful to the bad – for providing the world with a basis for comparison.

~ Sven Halla

Sincerity is an opening of the heart, found in very few people. What we usually see is merely a cunning deceit to gain another's confidence.

~ Francois, Duc de La Rochefoucauld

Conscience is a mother-in-law whose visit never ends.

~ H. L. Mencken

The test of a man or woman's breeding is how they behave in a quarrel.

~ George Bernard Shaw

What is a man profited if he shall gain the whole world, and lose his own soul?

~ Matthew 16:26

Nothing can be more readily disproved than the old saw, "You can't keep a good man down." Most human societies have been beautifully organized to keep good men down.

~ John W. Gardner

...the man of virtue will not seek to live at the expense of injuring their virtue. They will even sacrifice their lives to preserve their virtue.

~ Confucius

The way I see it, it doesn't matter what you believe just so you're sincere.

~ Charles M. Schulz

Who to himself is law no law doth need,
Offends no law, and is a king indeed.

~ George Chapman

Good kings are the only dangerous enemies that modern democracy has.

~ Oscar Wilde

I think that we should be men first, and subjects afterward. It is not so desirable to cultivate a respect for the law, so much as for the right.

~ Henry David Thoreau

Writing for a penny a word is ridiculous. If a man wants to make a million dollars, the best way would be to start a new religion.

~ L. Ron Hubbard

Do not do an immoral thing for moral reasons.

~ Thomas Hardy

Moderation in temper is always a virtue; but moderation in principle is always a vice.

~ Thomas Paine

Crime is the logical extension of the sort of behavior that is often considered perfectly respectable in legitimate business.

~ Robert Rice

People do not care how nobly they live, only how long, despite the fact that it is within everyone's reach to live nobly, but within no one's reach to live long.

~ Lucius Annaeus Seneca

No man, for any considerable period, can wear one face to himself, and another to the multitude, without finally getting bewildered as to which may be true.

~ Nathaniel Hawthorne

I'll tell you a big secret, my friend: Don't wait for the Last judgment. It happens every day.

~ Albert Camus

He has honor if he holds himself to an ideal of conduct though it is inconvenient, unprofitable, or dangerous to do so.

~ Walter Lippman

An American who can make money, invoke God, and be no better than his neighbor, has nothing to fear but truth itself.

~ Marya Mannes

Act only on that maxim which you can at the same time will to become a universal law.

~ Immanuel Kant

The trouble with the profit system has always been that it was highly unprofitable to most people.

~ E. B. White

Glory ought to be the consequence, not the motive of our actions.

~ Pliny the Younger

All men profess honesty as long as they can. To believe all men honest would be folly. To believe none so, is something worse.

~ John Quincy Adams

Everyone would like to behave like a pagan, with everyone else behaving like a Christian.

~ Albert Camus

We who use the term honor do not do so lightly.
Through all our trials and defeats that must stay constant.
We need to grip both our swords and principles tightly.
The pull to forsake beliefs is ever present.

It is not enough to succeed. Others must fail.

~ Gore Vidal

The people always have some champion whom they set over themselves and nurse into greatness.... This is the root from which a tyrant springs; at first, he is a protector.

~ Plato

If a law requires you to be the agent of injustice to another, then, I say, break the law.

~ Henry David Thoreau

The release of atomic energy has not created a new problem. It has merely made more urgent the necessity of solving an existing one.

~ Albert Einstein

The most mature type of moral reasoning is that in which right action is defined by self-chosen ethical principles...regardless of law and social agreement.

~ Lawrence Kohlberg

Actions lie louder than words.

~ Carolyn Wells

Speak to the child in the same tone of voice you would use with your best friend.

~ Margaret Skutch

Morals are an acquirement... no man is born with them.

~ Mark Twain

Man is the only animal that can remain on friendly terms with the victims he intends to eat until he eats them.

~ Samuel Butler

Is honor an archaic concept?
Is it becoming the appendix of the human mind?
Those who do value it seem suspect.
Seeing a *Catch-22* and a double-bind,
People fold instead of standing erect-
True honor is becoming difficult to find.

The best way to keep one's word is not to give it.

~ Napoleon I

Conscience is a cur that will let you get past it but that you cannot keep from barking.

~ Anonymous

Do not sacrifice your children on the altar of your principles.

~ Unknown

He who values principles and exercises control
Faces the omnipresent threat of adversity.
Perceived as odd, foolhardy, and droll,
Despite the failure of respect by his society,
By crushing the dice rather than letting them roll-
He can sleep at night sure of his integrity.

Patriotism is often an arbitrary veneration of real estate above principles.

~ George Jean Nathan

He who cheats with an oath acknowledges that he's afraid of his enemy, but that he thinks little of God.

~ Plutarch

They who provide wealth to their children but neglect to improve them in virtue do like those who feed their horses high, but never train them to be useful.

~ Socrates

It is better to be deceived by one's friends than to deceive them.

~ Johann Wolfgang von Goethe

There is just one way to bring up a child in the way he should go, and that is to travel that way yourself.

~ Abraham Lincoln

If it's morally wrong to kill anyone, then it's morally wrong to kill anyone. Period.

~ George Carlin

When you hear some men talk about their love of country, it's a sign they expect to be paid for it.

~ H. L. Mencken

I am the opposite of a warmonger. I tried to protect us. I have regret connected to Hiroshima. We should have dropped the bombs not on Hiroshima but in Tokyo Bay. Ten million Japanese would have seen the blast and nobody would have been hurt. With the Japanese seeing that, we could have ended the war without killing.

~ Edward Teller

There are few who will not disclose the private affairs of their friends when at a loss for conversational subjects.

~ Friedrich Nietzsche

There is no kind of dishonesty into which otherwise good people more easily and frequently fall than that of defrauding the government.

~ Benjamin Franklin

Morality ~ timeless, transcendental, absolute ~ stands in the sharpest possible contrast to freedom, which is transient, inconsistent and dependent on mere circumstance.

~Alan Wolfe

Nobody knows the age of the human race, but everybody agrees that it is old enough to know better.

~ Anonymous

The word 'politics' is derived from the word 'poly', meaning 'many', and the word 'ticks', meaning 'blood sucking parasites'.

~ Larry Hardiman

The end cannot justify the means for the simple and obvious reason that the means employed determine the nature of the ends produced.

~ Aldous Huxley

It is even harder for the average ape to believe that he has descended from man.

~ H. L. Mencken

It is dangerous for a national candidate to say things that people might remember.

~ Eugene McCarthy

Oaths are but words, and words but wind.

~ Samuel Butler

You can't say that civilization don't advance, however, for in every war they kill you in a new way.

~ Will Rogers

When men grow virtuous in their old age, they only make a sacrifice to God of the devil's leavings.

~ Alexander Pope

The law, in its majestic equality, forbids the rich as well as the poor to sleep under bridges, to beg in the streets, and to steal bread.

~ Anatole France

You pray in your distress and in your need; would that you might also pray in the fullness of your joy and in your days of abundance.

~ Kahlil Gibran

The least initial deviation from the truth is multiplied later a thousand fold.

~ Aristotle

Honesty is a good thing, but it is not profitable to its possessor unless it is kept under control.

~ Don Marquis

Whenever I hear anyone arguing for slavery, I feel a strong impulse to see it tried on him personally.

~ Abraham Lincoln

Behold the audacity of the hypocrite!
They escape the unquestioning eye of humanity,
But will these men fare so well before our Creator?
Will they indeed face the judgment of their vile vanity?
Is it nothing more than a halo on a Satyr?
The Just here on earth are rightfully sick of it!

It is said that power corrupts, but actually it's more true that power attracts the corruptible. The sane are usually attracted by other things than power.

~ David Brin

For many reasons, I believe true altruism is rare or oxymoronic. But do good~ by all means! Even if the reasons are selfish to some degree, the world becomes a better place as acts of good proliferate.

The omission of good is no less reprehensible than the commission of evil.

~ Plutarch

Men are equal; it is not birth but virtue that makes the difference.

~ Voltaire

When men are pure, laws are useless; when men are corrupt, laws are broken.

~ Benjamin Disraeli

Nearly all men can stand adversity, but if you want to test a man's character, give him power.

~ Abraham Lincoln

The foundation on which my true self has been built
Is shaky to the degree that the bricks forming it are lies.
Part of the bedrock supporting my pride is silt-
I want one to know only truth upon gazing in these
eyes.

In the arena of human life, the honors and rewards fall
to those who show their good qualities in action.

~ Aristotle

The man or woman who has money, without having
had to work for it, who has all the comforts of life,
without effort, and who saves his own soul and
perhaps the soul of somebody else, such an individual
is rare, very rare indeed.

~ Booker T. Washington

I do not begrudge billionaires or millionaires their
incomes as long as children's basic needs of food and
health and shelter and childcare and education are met.
But something's out of balance when the number of
millionaires in the 1980s almost doubled and the
number of poor children increased by three million...

~ Marian Wright Edelman

There is...only a single *categorical imperative* and it is this: Act only on that maxim through which you can at the same time will that it should become a universal law!

~ Edmund Burke

...the safest course is to do nothing against one's conscience. With this secret, we can enjoy life and have no fear from death.

~ Voltaire

Our repentance is not so much regret for the ill we have done as fear of the ill that may happen to us in consequence.

~ Francois, Duc de La Rochefoucauld

One has to spend so much time over-practicing their morality because of the fact that in that split-second when one is faced with a moral choice, countless factors that travel at the speed of electrical impulses are influencing one's decision. In the critical moment, if moral choice-making is not deeply engrained – I dare say non-negotiable – anxiety or fear will erode one's higher impulses.

STRENGTH & COURAGE

Unused power slips imperceptibly into the hands of another.

~ Konrad Heiden

Perfect courage means doing unwitnessed what we would be capable of with the world looking on.

~ Francois, Duc de La Rochefoucauld

Nothing is more despicable than respect based on fear.

~ Albert Camus

A new position of responsibility will usually show a man to be a far stronger creature than was supposed.

~ William James

The only prize much cared for by the powerful is power.   The prize of the general is not a bigger tent, but power.

~ Oliver Wendell Holmes, Jr.

No man should go through life without once experiencing healthy, even bored solitude in the wilderness, finding himself depending solely on himself and thereby learning his true and hidden strength.

~ Jack Kerouac

I know we're all going to die. There's three of us who are going to do something about it.

~ Thomas Burnett, by cell phone, from Flight 93 that crashed in the Pennsylvania woods on 9/11/2001.

The truth that many people never understand, until it is too late, is that the more you try to avoid suffering the more you suffer, because the smaller and more insignificant things begin to torture you in proportion to your fear of being hurt.

~ Thomas Merton

Anyone can hold the helm when the sea is calm.

~ Publilius Syrus

The whole history of the world is summed up in the fact that, when nations are strong, they are not always just, and when they wish to be just, they are no longer strong.

~ Winston Churchill

If we would be guided by the light of reason, we must let our minds be bold.

~ Louis Brandeis

He who fears he will suffer, already suffers because of his fear.

~ Michel de Montaigne

A mind that is safe, secure, is a bourgeois mind, a shoddy mind. Yet that is what all of us want: to be completely safe.

~ J. Krishamurti

A leader or a man of action in a crisis almost always acts subconsciously and then thinks of the reasons for his actions.

~ Jawaharlal Nehru

Frodo: 'I wish the ring had never come to me. I wish none of this had happened.'
Gandalf: 'So do all who live to see such times. But it is not for them to decide. All you have to decide is what to do with the time that is given to you.'

~ J.R.R. Tolkien

I do not wish to treat friendships daintily, but with the roughest courage. When they are real, they are not glass thread or frostwork, but the solidest thing we know.

~ Ralph Waldo Emerson

The darkness has a hunger that's insatiable. And the lightness has a call that's hard to hear. So I wrap my fear around me like a blanket; I sail my ship of safety until I sank it.

~ Emily Saliers, Amy Ray

Independence is for the very few; it is a privilege of the strong.

~ Friedrich Nietzsche

The most effective way to ensure the value of the future is to confront the present courageously and constructively.

~ Rollo May

The probability that we shall fail in the struggle should not deter us from the support of a cause we believe to be just.

~ Abraham Lincoln

Happiness is a form of courage.

~ Holbrook Jackson

You can listen to what everybody says, but the fact remains that you've got to get out there and do the thing yourself.

~ Joan Sutherland

Every man who is truly a man must learn to be alone in the midst of all the others, and if need be against all the others.

~ Romain Rolland

Courage is the most important of all the virtues, because without it we can't practice any other virtue with consistency.

~ Maya Angelou

If we take the generally accepted definition of bravery as a quality when knows not fear, I have never seen a brave man. All men are frightened. The more intelligent they are, the more they are frightened. The courageous man is the man who forces himself, in spite of his fear, to carry on. Discipline, pride, self-respect, self-confidence, and the love of glory are attributes which will make a man courageous even when he is afraid.

~ George S. Patton, Jr.

Parents learn a lot from their children about coping with life.

~ Muriel Spark

Rudeness is the weak man's imitation of strength.

~ Eric Hoffer

I preach to you, then, my countrymen, that our country calls not for the life of ease, but for the life of strenuous endeavor. The twentieth century looms before us big with the fate of many nations. If we stand idly by, if we seek merely swollen, slothful ease, and ignoble peace, if we shrink from the hard contests where men must win at hazard of their lives and at risk of all they hold dear, then the bolder and stronger peoples will pass us by and win for themselves the domination of the world.

Let us therefore boldly face the life of strife, resolute to do our duty well and manfully; resolute to uphold righteousness by deed and by word; resolute to be both honest and brave, to serve high ideals, yet to use practical methods. Above all, let us shrink from no strife, moral or physical, within or without the nation, provided we are certain that the strife is justified; for it is only through strife, through hard work and dangerous endeavor, that we shall ultimately win the goal of true national greatness.

~ Theodore Roosevelt

One may go a long way after one is tired.

~ French proverb

Let us never negotiate out of fear, but let us never fear to negotiate.

~ John F. Kennedy

Fall seven times, stand up eight.

~ Japanese proverb

At times, our strengths propel us so far forward we can no longer endure our weaknesses and perish from them.

~ Friedrich Nietzsche

I am glad to see that men are getting their rights, but I want women to get theirs, and while the water is stirring I will step into the pool.

~ Sojourner Truth

A man can stand a lot as long as he can stand himself. He can live without hope, without friends, without books, even without music, as long as he can listen to his own thoughts.

~ Axel Munthe

Every man must bear his own burden.

~ Galatians 6:5

No man can honestly think of himself as a strong character because, however successful he may be in overcoming them, he is necessarily aware of the doubts and temptations that accompany every important choice.

~ W. H. Auden

If we are strong, our character will speak for itself. If we are weak, words will be of no help.

~ John F. Kennedy

There are three things a man must do alone. Be born, die, and testify.

~ James J. Walker

To penetrate one's being, one must go armed to the teeth.

~ Paul Valery

Nobody knows what's in him until he tries to pull it out. If there's nothing, or very little, the shock can kill a man.

~ Ernest Hemmingway

There are several good protections against temptation, but the surest is cowardice.

~ Mark Twain

Deliberation is the work of many men. Action, of one alone.

~ Charles de Gaulle

Man who man would be, must rule the empire of himself.

~ Percy Bysshe Shelley

It is a great shock to find at the age of 5 or 6 that in a world of Gary Coopers you are the Indian.

~ James Baldwin

The absence of alternatives clears the mind marvelously.

~ Henry Kissinger

One of the greatest contributors to that so-called "fatal" mentality that is a part of me is the notion that, if I am called to duty and fail to act when I ought to have, what good is my life? How many times can one forgo opportunities to uphold one's cherished beliefs and still have a self-image as a "good" person?

Force is never more operative than when it is known to exist but is not brandished.

~ Alfred Thayer Mahan

Power never takes a back step – only in the face of more power.

~ Malcolm X

People exercise an unconscious selection in being influenced.

~ T. S. Eliot

The courage of the poet is to keep ajar the door that leads into madness.

~ Christopher Morley

Each man must for himself alone decide what is right and what is wrong, which course is patriotic and which isn't. You cannot shirk this and be a man.

~ Mark Twain

There are two ways to slide easily through life; to believe everything or doubt everything. Both ways save us from thinking.

~ Alfred Korzybski

Man is a gregarious animal, and much more so in his mind than in his body. He may like to go for a walk alone, but he hates to stand alone in his opinions.

~ George Santyana

Thunder is good, thunder is impressive; but it is the lightening that does the work.

~ Mark Twain

Patience has limits. Take it too far, and it's cowardice.

~ George Jackson

Pessimism is only the name that men of weak nerves give to wisdom.

~ Elbert Hubbard

The chain of wedlock is so heavy that it takes two to carry it – sometimes three.

~ Alexandre Dumas

You don't learn to hold your own by standing on guard, but by attacking, and getting well hammered yourself.

~ George Bernard Shaw

Life as we find it is too hard for us; it entails too much pain, too many disappointments, impossible tasks. We cannot do without palliative remedies.

~ Sigmund Freud

Weak people cannot be sincere.

> ~ Francois, Duc de La Rochefoucauld

In the midst of winter, I finally learned that there was in me an invincible summer.

> ~ Albert Camus

Maturity is the capacity to endure uncertainty.

> ~ John Finley

What we can do for another is the test of powers; what we can suffer is the test of love.

> ~ Brooke Foss Wescott

Conscience gets a lot of credit that belongs to cold feet.

> ~ Anonymous

Well-behaved women rarely make history.

> ~ Laurel Thatcher Ulrich

The lonely one offers his hand too quickly to whomever he encounters.

~ Friedrich Nietzsche

He alone deserves liberty and life who daily must win them anew.

~ Johann Wolfgang von Goethe

We are all afraid – for our confidence, for the future, for the world.... Yet every man, every civilization, has gone forward because of its engagement with what it has set itself to do.

~ Jacob Bronowski

Everything I did in my life that was worthwhile I caught hell for.

~ Earl Warren

The hottest places in hell are reserved for those who, in time of great moral crisis, maintain their neutrality.

~ Dante Aligheri

The art of living is more like that of wrestling than of dancing. The main thing is to stand firm and be ready for an unseen attack.

~ Marcus Aurelius

Only the wise possess ideas; the greater part of mankind are possessed by them.

~ Samuel Taylor Coleridge

The highest and loftiest trees have the most reason to dread the thunder.

~ Charles Rollin

To be a leader of men one must turn one's back on men.

~ Havelock Ellis

The last thing a woman will consent to discover in a man whom she loves, or on whom she simply depends, is want of courage.

~ Joseph Conrad

One man with courage makes a majority.

~ Andrew Jackson

Great men, great nations, have not been boasters and buffoons, but perceivers of the terror of life, and have manned themselves to meet it.

~ Ralph Waldo Emerson

The weakest and most timorous are the most revengeful and implacable.

~ Thomas Fuller

Oh, you weak, beautiful people who give up with such grace. What you need is someone to take hold of you – gently, with love, and hand your life back to you.

~ Tennessee Williams

Courage is fear holding on a minute longer.

~ George S. Patton

We must be ready to dare all for our country. For history does not long entrust the care of freedom to the weak or the timid.

~ Dwight D. Eisenhower

He who is outside his door already has the hard part of his journey behind him.

~ Dutch proverb

Courage! I have shown it for years; think you I shall lose it at the moment when my sufferings are about to end?

~ Marie Antoinette

War is an unmitigated evil. But it certainly does one thing: It drives away fear and brings bravery to the surface.

~ Mohandas K. Gandhi

When you appeal to force, there is one thing you must never do – lose.

~ Dwight D. Eisenhower

Conscience does make cowards of us all.

~ William Shakespeare

Some people mistake weakness for tact. If they are silent when they ought to speak and so feign an agreement they do not feel, they call it being tactful. Cowardice would be a much better name.

~ Frank Medlicott

I will permit no man to narrow and degrade my soul by making me hate him.

~ Booker T. Washington

Nobody can give you freedom. Nobody can give you equality or justice or anything. If you're a man, you take it.

~ Malcolm X

The thought of suicide is a powerful comfort: it helps one through many a dreadful night.

~ Friedrich Nietzsche

We confide in our strength, without boasting of it; we respect that of others, without fearing it.

~ Thomas Jefferson

My head was exploding, my stomach ripping, and even the tips of my fingers ached. The only thing I think I could think was, "If I live, I will never run again."

~ Tom Courtney

Religion will not gain its old power until it can face change in the same spirit as does science.

~ Alfred North Whitehead

If we would guide by the light of reason, we must let our minds be bold.

~ Louis Brandeis

One doesn't discover new lands without consenting to lose sight of the shore for a very long time.

~ Andre Gide

'Tis man's perdition to be safe,
When for the truth he ought to die.

~ Ralph Waldo Emerson

To escape criticism - do nothing, say nothing, be nothing.

~ Elbert Hubbard

He that struggles with us strengthens our nerves, and sharpens our skill. Our antagonist is our helper.

~ Edmund Burke

Leadership is more likely to be assumed by the aggressive than the able, and those who scramble to the top are more often motivated by their own inner torments.

~ Bergen Evans

Serving one's own passions is the greatest slavery.

~ T. S. Eliot

To conquer fear is the beginning of wisdom.

~ Bertrand Russell

In love there are no vacations.... No such thing. Love has to be lived fully with its boredom and all that.

~ Marguerite Duras

One must raise the self by the self
And not let the self sink down,
For the self's only friend is the self
And the self is the self's one enemy.

~ Bhagavad-Gita

Unquestionably, it is possible to do without happiness; it is done involuntarily by nineteen-twentieths of mankind.

~ John Stuart Mill

Learn to say no. It will be more use to you than to able to read Latin.

~ Charles Spurgeon

Resistance to tyrants is obedience to God.

~ Thomas Jefferson

Danger and dishonor come in all shapes and sizes.
Desperation drives one to literally fight or flee.
Challenges have many faces and varied guises-
Emulate the undaunted falcon or steadfast oak tree...

It is easier to believe than to doubt.

~ E. D. Martin

The Negro was willing to risk martyrdom in order to
move and stir the social conscience of...the nation...
He would force his oppressor to commit his brutality
openly, with the rest of the world looking on.

~ Martin Luther King, Jr.

There is in every true woman's heart a spark of
heavenly fire, which lies dormant in the broad daylight
of prosperity; but which kindles up, and beams and
blazes in the dark hour of adversity.

~ Washington Irving

The paradox of courage is that man must be a little careless of his life even in order to keep it.

~ G. K. Chesterton

Life shrinks or expands in proportion to one's courage.

~ Anais Nin

Lisa Beamer, the widow of American patriot Todd Beamer, who died attacking the would-be destroyers of the White House on Flight 93 on 9-11-2001, subsequently found this quote of Teddy Roosevelt while going through Todd's desk: 'The credit belongs to the man who is actually in the arena...who strives valiantly, who knows the great enthusiasms, the great devotions, and spends himself in worthy causes. Who, at best, knows the triumph of high achievement and who, at worst, if he fails, fails while daring greatly so that his place shall never be with those cold and timid souls who know neither victory nor defeat.'

Can we raise our eyes and make a start?
Can we find the minds to lead us *closer to the heart*?

~ Neil Peart

The weak can never forgive.   Forgiveness is the attribute of the strong.

~ Mohandas K. Gandhi

Nothing is so strong as gentleness; nothing so gentle as real strength.

~ Francis de Sales

Anything connected to war is wrong in some people's opinion. But there is a Latin statement: If you wish for peace, prepare for war.

~ Edward Teller

Throughout the whole of life one must continue to learn to live, and what will amaze you even more, throughout life one must learn to die.

~ Lucius Annaeus Seneca

Have something to say; say it, and stop when you're done.

~ Tryon Edwards

A good soldier is not violent. A good fighter is not angry.

~ Lao Tsu

Pain nourishes courage. You can't be brave if you've only had good things happen to you.

~ Mary Tyler Moore

Sometimes the noble knight must fight alone,
His brothers in arms being bested all around.
Of course he feels that fear down to the bone,
But his courage and duty keep him bearing down...

The best decision makers are those who are willing to suffer the most over their decisions but still retain the ability to be decisive.

~ M. Scott Peck

You can't shake hands with a clenched fist.

~ Indira Gandhi

We all take different paths in life, but no matter where we go, we take a little of each other everywhere.

~ Tim McGraw

Tenderness and kindness are not signs of weakness and despair, but manifestations of strength and resolutions

~ Kahlil Gibran

Better to die on your feet than to live on your knees.

~ Euripides

There are times when we are called to duty~
Necessity dictates revolutionary action.
The time comes when we must stand and be counted~
Proactivity arises from the place of reaction.

Oh, father of the four winds, fill my sails, across the sea of years,
With no provision but an open face, along the straits of fear...

~ John Bonham, John Paul Jones,
Jimmy Page, Robert Plant

Question with boldness even the existence of a god;
because if there be one he must approve of the homage
of reason more than that of blindfolded fear.

~ Thomas Jefferson

The strong must herald the banner of the weak;
The good champion the rights of the innocent.
Only the truly noble man helps the meek;
Standing courageously makes us magnificent...

If an act is not one of work or courage, then it is not an
act of love.

~ M. Scott Peck

Sometimes I think we're alone.   Sometimes I think
we're not.   In either case, the thought is staggering.

~ Buckminster Fuller

Why not go out on a limb? Isn't that where the fruit is?

~ Frank Scully

The fear of death is more to be dreaded than death itself.

~ Publilius Syrus

Men fear thought as they fear nothing else on earth...even more than death.

~ Bertrand Russell

The best decision makers are those who are willing to suffer the most over their decisions but still retain the ability to be decisive.

~ M. Scott Peck

The only thing necessary for the triumph of evil is for good men to do nothing.

~ Johann Fichte

Small is the number of them that see with their own eyes and feel with their own hearts.

~ Albert Einstein

Beware the fury of a patient man.

~ John Dryden

Dare to do things worthy of imprisonment if you mean to be of consequence.

~ Juvenal

I have often asked myself whether I am not more heavily obligated to the hardest years of my life than to any others. As my inmost nature teaches me, whatever is necessary as seen from the heights and in the sense of a great economy is also the useful par excellence: one should not only bear it, one should love it. *Amor fati*: that is my inmost nature. And as for my long sickness, do I not owe it indescribably more than I owe to my health? I owe it a higher health one which is made stronger by whatever does not kill it. I also owe my philosophy to it. Only great pain is the ultimate liberator of the spirit.... Only great pain, that long, slow pain in which we are burned with green wood, as it were - pain which takes its time ~ only this forces us philosophers to descend into our ultimate depths and to put away all trust, all good-naturedness, all that would veil, all mildness, all that is medium ~ things in which formerly we may have found our humanity. I doubt that such a pain makes us "better," but I know that it makes us more profound.

~ Friedrich Nietzsche

If you can't bite, don't show your teeth.

~ Yiddish proverb

If you don't want to be criticized, don't say anything, do anything, or be anything.

~ Anonymous

Slowly, she changed my view of the world...
Countless phone conversations meant so much...
Our consonant views of our future aspirations...
More than I miss her eyes, I miss her touch.

Sometimes even to live is an act of courage.

~ Lucius Annaeus Seneca

One sword keeps another in the sheath.

~ George Herbert

Waste not fresh tears over old griefs.

~ Euripides

153

A very popular error – having the courage of one's convictions. Rather it is a matter of having the courage for an attack upon one's convictions.

~ Friedrich Nietzsche

An appeaser is one who feeds a crocodile, hoping that it will eat him last.

~ Winston Churchill

He knows not his own strength that hath not met adversity.

~ Ben Jonson

FULFILLMENT, MEANING & HOPE

To love what you do and feel that it matters – how could anything be more fun?

~ Katharine Graham

Grief drives men into habits of serious reflection, sharpens the understanding, and softens the heart.

~ John Adams

An unfulfilled vocation drains the color from a man's entire existence.

~ Honore de Balzac

Happiness is found doing, not merely possessing.

~ Napoleon Hill

What sort of philosophy one chooses depends, therefore, on what sort of man one is; for a philosophical system is not a dead piece of furniture that we can reject or accept as we wish; it is rather a thing animated by the soul of the person who holds it.

~ Friedrich Nietzsche

Our scientific power has outrun our spiritual power. We have guided missiles and misguided men.

~ Martin Luther King Jr.

Science without religion is lame, religion without science is blind.

~ Albert Einstein

The orgasm has replaced the cross as the focus of longing and the image of fulfillment.

~ Malcolm Muggeridge

Man has to suffer. When he has no real afflictions, he invents some.

~ Jose Marti

A person will be called to account on Judgment Day for every permissible thing he might have enjoyed but did not.

~ The Talmud

The real reason for not committing suicide is because you always know how swell life gets again after the hell is over.

~ Ernest Hemingway

Our greatest pretenses are built up not to hide the evil and the ugly in us, but our emptiness. The hardest thing to hide is something that is not there.

~ Eric Hoffer

Time is short for one who thinks, endless for one who yearns.

~ Alain

Life is a long preparation for something that never happens.

~ William Butler Yeats

157

The mark of your ignorance is the depth of your belief in injustice and tragedy. What the caterpillar calls the end of the world, the master calls a butterfly.

~ Richard Bach

There is no cure for birth or death save to enjoy the interval.

~ George Santyana

We have survived everything, and we have only survived it on our optimism.

~ Edward Steichen

Hope is the pillar that holds up the world. Hope is the dream of the waking man.

~ Pliny the Elder

The more one suffers, the more, I believe, one has a sense of the comic. It is only by the deepest suffering that one acquires the authority in the art of the comic.

~ Soren Kierkegaard

Finding meaning in one's avocation, one's pursuit – consists of determining what one's special area of intelligence or intrigue is, and marrying that to the engine of passion to fuel its motion as though one was finding a pleasing racetrack and flooring the gas pedal.

He that wrestles with us strengthens our nerves and sharpens our skill. Our antagonist is our helper.

~ Edmund Burke

Great minds have purposes, others have wishes.

~ Washington Irving

Continuity of purpose is one of the most essential ingredients of happiness in the long run, and for most men this comes chiefly through their work.

~ Bertrand Russell

Comedy is an escape, not from truth but from despair; a narrow escape into faith.

~ Christopher Fry

I'd like to live like a poor man with lots of money.

~ Pablo Picasso

Money is necessary – both to support a family and to advance causes one believes in.

~ Coretta Scott King

It may be life is only worthwhile at moments. Perhaps that is all we ought to expect.

~ Sherwood Anderson

True love is a discipline in which each divines the secret self of the other and refuses to believe in the mere daily self.

~ William Butler Yeats

There is precious little hope to be got out of whatever keeps us industrious, but there is a chance for us whenever we cease work and become stargazers.

~ H. M. Tomlinson

More are taken in by hope than by cunning.

~ Luc de Clapiers de Vauvenargues

Making money is easy; knowing what to do with it becomes a problem.

~ Ring Lardner

Prayer does not change God, but changes he who prays.

~ Soren Kierkegaard

People are hungry for a hero, one who fits the new age.... A good deal is riding on the question whether they will find a demagogue or a democrat as they search out a way to link their passions to their government.

~ James David Barber

The soul is made for action, and cannot rest 'till it be employed.

~ Thomas Traherne

One joy scatters a hundred griefs.

~ Chinese proverb

Everybody needs his memories. They keep the wolf of insignificance from the door.

~ Saul Bellow

The tragedy of life is not so much what men suffer, but rather what they miss.

~ Thomas Carlyle

If only men could be induced to laugh more they might hate less, and find more serenity here on earth.

~ Malcolm Muggeridge

Yes, there is a Nirvana; it is leading your sheep to a green pasture, and in putting your child to sleep, and in writing the last line of your poem.

~ Kahlil Gibran

This is the true joy in life: being used for a purpose recognized by yourself as a mighty one.

~ George Bernard Shaw

Laziness is nothing more than the habit of resting before you get tired.

~ Jules Renard

The mind which renounces, once and forever, a futile hope, has its compensation in ever-growing calm.

~ George Gissing

It's pretty hard to tell what does bring happiness. Poverty and wealth have both failed.

~ Kin Hubbard

I know what things are good: friendship, work, and conversation. These I shall have.

~ Rupert Brooke

An object in possession seldom retains the same charm it had in pursuit.

~ Pliny the Younger

Anything you're good at contributes to happiness.

~ Bertrand Russell

The greater the difficulty the more glory in surmounting it.

~ Epicurus

I urge you to view your inevitable demise not with grief or fear but with acceptance and perhaps even hope. Your death is an end to sadness and pain. Your death is a passage to a better world. Your death is a moment of unification with the sacredness of eternity. My death, on the other hand? Greatest fuckin' tragedy in the history of mankind.

~ Dennis Miller

Wisdom comes alone through suffering.

~ Aeschylus

164

It gives one a sense of freedom to know that anyone in this world can really do a deliberately courageous act.

~ Henrik Ibsen

Duty does not have to be dull. Love can make it beautiful and fill it with life.

~ Thomas Merton

As long as there is one upright man, as long as there is one compassionate woman, the contagion may spread and the scene is not desolate. Hope is the thing that is left to us in a bad time.

~ E. B. White

Sweet is the memory of distant friends! Like the mellow rays of the departing sun, it falls tenderly, yet sadly, on the heart.

~ Washington Irving

The limits of my language are the limits of my mind. All I know is what I have words for.

~ Ludwig Wittgenstein

Letter-writing is the only device for combining solitude with good company.

~ Lord Byron

Out of every fruition of success, no matter what, comes forth something to make a new effort necessary.

~ Walt Whitman

Unhurt people are not much good in the world.

~ Enid Starkie

Blessed are they who heal us of self-despising. Of all services which can be done to man, I know of none more precious.

~ William Hale White

A good poem is a contribution to reality. The world is never the same once a good poem has been added to it. A good poem helps to change the shape and significance of the universe, helps to extend everyone's knowledge of himself and the world around him.

~ Dylan Thomas

Most people work the greater part of their time for a mere living; and the little freedom which remains to them so troubles them that they use every means of getting rid of it.

~ Johann Wilhelm von Goethe

I must take issue with the term 'a mere child,' for it has been my invariable experience that the company of a mere child is infinitely preferable to that of a mere adult.

~ Fran Lebowitz

You must not count overmuch on your reality as you feel it today, since, like that of yesterday, it may prove an illusion for you tomorrow.

~ Luigi Pirandello

Religion converts despair, which destroys, into resignation, which submits.

~ Lady Blessington

Amusement is the happiness of those that cannot think.

~ Alexander Pope

The quest for certainty blocks the search for meaning. Uncertainty is the very condition to impel man to unfold his powers.

~ Erich Fromm

Should you shield the canyons from the windstorms you would never see the true beauty of their carvings.

~ Elisabeth Kubler-Ross

Employment is nature's physician, and is essential to human happiness.

~ Galen

Three passions, simple but overwhelmingly strong, have governed my life: the longing for love, the search for knowledge, and unbearable pity for the suffering of mankind.

~ Bertrand Russell

In much wisdom is much grief: and he that increaseth knowledge increaseth sorrow.

~ Ecclesiastes 1:18

And from the discontent of man
The world's best progress springs.

~ Ella Wheeler Wilcox

Melancholy men are of all others the wittiest.

~ Aristotle

Romanticism is the expression of man's urge to rise above reason and common sense, just as rationalism is the expression of his urge to rise above theology and emotion.

~ Charles Yost

We all live with the objective of being happy: our lives are all different and yet the same.

~ Anne Frank

There's no money in poetry, but then there's no poetry in money either.

~ Robert Graves

When I was young, I used to think that wealth and power would bring me happiness... I was right.

~ Gahan Wilson

The fundamental defect of fathers is that they want their children to be a credit to them.

~ Bertrand Russell

When people hear good music, it makes them homesick for something they never had, and never will have.

~ Edgar Watson Howe

The entire sum of existence is the magic of being needed by just one person.

~ Vi Putnam

Poverty sits by the cradle of all our great men and rocks all of them to manhood.

~ Heinrich Heine

Where the mind is past hope, the heart is past shame.

~ John Lyly

Parents are the bones on which children cut their teeth.

~ Peter Ustinov

Lives based on having are less free than lives based either on doing or being.

~ William James

When it's dark enough, you can see the stars.

~ Charles A. Beard

Adversity's sweet milk, philosophy.

~ William Shakespeare

The tyrant dies and his rule is over; the martyr dies and his rule begins.

~ Soren Kierkegaard

The feeling of inferiority rules the mental life and can be clearly recognized as the sense of incompleteness and unfulfillment, and in the uninterrupted struggle both of individuals and of humanity.

~ Alfred Adler

No love, no friendship can cross the path of our destiny without leaving some mark on it forever.

~ Francois Mauriac

There is not enough darkness in all the world to put out the light of even one small candle.

~ Robert Alden

He who has a why to live can bear with almost any how.

~ Friedrich Nietzsche

The good life, as I conceive it, is a happy life. I do not mean that if you are good you will be happy – I mean that if you are happy you will be good.

~ Bertrand Russell

My religion consists of a humble admiration of the illimitable superior spirit who reveals himself in the slight details we are able to perceive with our frail and feeble mind.

~ Albert Einstein

He who despairs of the human condition is a coward, but he who has hope for it is a fool.

~ Albert Camus

The value of a sentiment is the amount of sacrifice you are prepared to make for it.

~ John Galsworthy

The effort to understand the universe is one of the very few things that lifts human life a little above the level of farce, and gives it some of the grace of tragedy.

~ Steven Weinberg

For what human ill does not dawn seem to be an alleviation?

~ Thornton Wilder

Unto whomsoever much is given, of him shall much be required.

~ Luke 12:48

One of the best safeguards of hope is to be able to mark off the areas of hopelessness and to acknowledge them, to face them directly, not with despair, but with the creative intent of keeping them from polluting all the areas of possibility.

~ William F. Lynch

No man is a failure who is enjoying life.

~ William Feather

Experience is not what happens to a man. It is what a man does with what happens to him.

~ Aldous Huxley

There are two things to aim at in life: first, to get what you want, and after that to enjoy it.

~ Logan Pearsall Smith

Most people do not believe in anything very much and our greatest poetry is given to us by those that do.

~ Cyril Connolly

To really enjoy the better things in life, one must first have experienced the things they are better than.

~ Oscar Homolka

The best-educated human being is the one who understands the most about the life in which he is placed.

~ Helen Keller

There is more to life than increasing its speed.

~ Mohandas K. Gandhi

Hope is a pleasant acquaintance, but an unsafe friend.

~ Thomas Haliburton

What really raises one's indignation against suffering is not suffering intrinsically, but the senselessness of suffering.

~ Friedrich Nietzsche

Is not marriage an open question, when it is alleged, from the beginning of the world, that such as are in the institution wish to get out, and such as are out wish to get in?

~ Ralph Waldo Emerson

To be a man is to feel that one's own stone contributes to building the edifice of the world.

~ Antoine de Saint-Exupery

Where, unwilling, dies the rose,
Buds the new, another year.

~ Dorothy Parker

Time heals grief and quarrels, for we change and are no longer the same person.

~ Blaise Pascal

With the fearful strain that is on me night and day, if I did not laugh I should die.

~ Abraham Lincoln

Nobody can have the consolations of religion or philosophy unless he has first experienced their desolations.

~ Aldous Huxley

Mankind will never see an end of trouble until...lovers of wisdom come to hold political power, or the holders of power...become lovers of wisdom.

~ Plato

There is a secret person undamaged in every individual.

~ Paul Shepard

To a poet nothing can be useless.

~ Samuel Johnson

...my views regarding liberal studies... I deem no study good which results in money-making.

~ Lucius Annaeus Seneca

The lover is a monotheist who knows that other people worship different gods but cannot himself imagine that there could be other gods.

~ Theodor Reik

Live all you can; it's a mistake not to. It doesn't matter so much what you do in particular, so long as you're living your life. If you haven't had that, what have you had?

~ Henry James

Hold it the greatest wrong to prefer life to honor and for the sake of life to lose the reason for living.

~ Juvenal

The past can be remembered with a smile or downcast eyes, with the difference being one's attitude.

A proverb is no proverb to you 'till life has illustrated it.

~ John Keats

How remarkable it is
To transcend *mundaneness!*
To enter "the flow,"
To feel her soft kiss.

He is rich that is satisfied.

~ Thomas Fuller

Ideals are like the stars; you will not succeed in touching them with your hands. But like the seafaring man on the desert of waters, you choose them as your guides, and following them you will reach your destiny.

~ Carl Schurz

If you can find a path with no obstacles, it probably doesn't lead anywhere.

~ Frank A. Clark

Literature is my Utopia. Here I am not disfranchised.

~ Helen Keller

Who hears music, feels his solitude peopled at once.

~ Robert Browning

Nothing contributes so much to tranquilize the mind as a steady purpose – a point on which the soul may fix its intellectual eye.

~ Mary Wollenstonecraft

Why not strive for joie de vivre,
Beyond a life bereft of fervor?
Why not decide to *believe*,
Thus taking you higher and further?

If we had no winter, the spring would not be so pleasant; if we did not sometimes taste of adversity, prosperity would not be so welcome.

~ Anne Bradstreet

It is better to be a human dissatisfied than a pig satisfied, better Socrates than a fool satisfied.

~ John Stuart Mill

The chief value of money lies in the fact that one lives in a world in which it is overestimated.

~ H. L. Mencken

Love is as powerful as profit.

All I can do is to urge you to put friendship ahead of all other human concerns, for there is nothing so suited to man's nature, nothing that can mean so much to him, whether in good times or in bad... I am inclined to think that with the exception of wisdom, the gods have given nothing finer to men than this.

~ Marcus Tullius Cicero

Man is the only animal for whom his own existence is a problem which he has to solve.

~ Erich Fromm

Still around the corner may wait,
A new road, or a secret gate.

~ J.R.R. Tolkien

The avoidance of taxes is the only intellectual pursuit that carries any reward.

~ John Maynard Keynes

My life has no purpose, no direction, no aim, no meaning, and yet I'm happy. I can't figure it out. What am I doing right?

~ Charles M. Schulz

When I despair, I remember that all through history, the way of truth and love has always won. There have been tyrants and murderers, and for a time they have seemed invincible, but in the end, they always fall. Think of it: always.

~ Mohandas K. Gandhi

Aspirations are as laudable as possessions.

A breath of fresh air is afforded by knowledge,
By experiencing life and classes at college.
Seize the day or don't bother trying;
Get busy living or get busy dying!
(last line from Steven King)

As a day well-spent brings a happy sleep, so a life well used brings happy death.

~ Leonardo da Vinci

Physics, astronomical phenomena, microbiology, and on and on...
Are masked in darkness until our senses or reason bring the dawn.
Yet we have no direct evidence of God;
Perhaps one day the skeptical will be awed....

The more I study religions the more I am convinced that man never worshipped anything but himself.

~ Sir Richard Francis Burton

There is a budding morrow in midnight.

~ John Keats

As the American spirit teeters between rage and compassion, pray we tip toward compassion and take the world with us.

~ Geraldine Laybourne

The absence of a sense of purpose unifying mankind is upon us.
Mental laziness and emotional immaturity mark present-day earth.
Inadequate legal constraints failing to make up for a dearth of trust.
Can we find in human hearts the means to create a spiritual rebirth?

Seek ye first the good things of the mind, and the rest will either be supplied or its loss will not be felt.

~ Francis Bacon

Whatever does not destroy me makes me stronger.

~ Friedrich Nietzsche

When the well's dry, we know the worth of the water.

~ Benjamin Franklin

Music, the greatest good that mortals know,
And all of heaven we have below.

~ Joseph Addison

Everyone whose deeds are more than his wisdom, his wisdom endures. And everyone whose wisdom is more than his deeds, his wisdom does not endure.

~ The Talmud

The finer things in life are fine, but the meaningful things in life are more meaningful.

The activity of happiness must occupy an entire lifetime; for one swallow does not a summer make.

~Aristotle

Seek always to do some good, somewhere. Every man has to seek in his own way to make his self more noble and to realize his own true worth.

~ Albert Schweitzer

A radiant full moon reflects the faraway sun's beatific smile,
Warm breezes blow across California's lonesome plain,
The silence of plastic suburbs of this pseudo Utopia.
This hollow existence engenders a slight sense of pain.

And forget not that the earth delights to feel your bare feet and the winds long to play with your hair.

~ Kahlil Gibran

The great art of life is sensation, to feel that we exist, even in pain.

~ Lord Byron

God never meant to make life easy, he meant to make humans great.

~ Unknown

DEVELOPMENT, PROGRESSIVISM & INTEGRATION

Few men make themselves masters of the things they write or speak.

~ John Selden

I can feel guilty about the past, apprehensive about the future, but only in the present can I act. The ability to be in the present moment is a major component of mental wellness.

~ Abraham Maslow

Some things about ourselves have to be exercised, others exorcised.

~ Tanya Dunn

Our deeds still travel with us from afar, and what we have been makes us what we are.

~ George Eliot

Congruence between experience and self-concept is a healthy personality.

~ Carl Rogers

It is never too late to give up our prejudices.

~ Henry David Thoreau

A certain talent is indispensable for people who would spend years together and not bore each other to death.

~ Robert Louis Stevenson

To the question whether I am a pessimist or an optimist, I answer that my knowledge is pessimistic, but my will and hope are optimistic.

~ Albert Schweitzer

Equilibrium is the profoundest tendency of all human activity.

~ Jean Piaget

It is a melancholy truth that even great men have their poor relationships.

~ Charles Dickens

All human things are subject to decay,
And when fate summons, monarchs must obey.

~ John Dryden

A thousand things advance; nine hundred and ninety-nine retreat; that is progress.

~ Henri Frederic Amiel

Despite all efforts, things are badly ordered for the soul in human society.

~ Alfred Adler

All things flow, nothing abides.

~ Heraclitus

To conquer oneself is a greater task than conquering others.

~ Buddha

The trouble is that everyone talks about reforming others, and no one thinks about reforming himself.

~ Saint Peter of Alcantara

The human can control his own evolution, to some degree, maybe.

~ Murray Bowen

As a Mexican, I always look to America as an example of what freedom means. As a Jew, I always admired how this country accepted and respected our traditions and beliefs. Now, as an American citizen, I'm proud to be a part of a nation that stands together, looking toward the future, with dignity and strength.

~ Pepe Stepensky

Each needs to develop the sides of his personality which he has neglected.

~ Alexis Carrel

The past is not a package one can lay away.

~ Emily Dickinson

To teach a man how he may grow independently, and for himself, is perhaps the greatest service that one man can do for another.

~ Benjamin Jowett

One cannot too soon forget his errors and misdemeanors; for to dwell upon them is to add to the offense.

~ Henry David Thoreau

The value and force of a man's judgment can be measured by his ability to think independently of his temperamental leanings.

~ Algernon S. Logan

You must do the thing you think you cannot do.

~ Eleanor Roosevelt

To philosophize is to explore one's own temperament, yet at the same time to attempt to discover the truth

~ Iris Murdoch

The man who is too old to learn was probably always too old to learn.

~ Henry S. Haskins

It is in his pleasure that a man really lives; it is from his leisure that he constructs the true fabric of self.

~ Agnes Repplier

It isn't the burdens of today that drive men mad. It is the regrets over yesterday and the fear of tomorrow. Regret and fear are twin thieves who rob us of today.

~ Robert J. Hastings

Nature takes away any faculty that is not used.

~ William R. Inge

Not only is it hard to be a man, it is harder to become one.

~ Arianna Stassinopolous

It requires greater courage to preserve inner freedom, to move on in one's inward journey into new realms, than to stand defiantly for outer freedom.

~ Rollo May

There must always be a struggle between a father and a son, while one aims at power the other at independence.

~ Samuel Johnson

Unless I accept my faults I will most certainly doubt my virtues.

~ Hugh Prather

The world belongs to the enthusiast who keeps cool.

~ William McFee

Enjoy when you can, and endure when you must.

~ Johann Wolfgang von Goethe

Anything that can be done chemically can be done in other ways – that is, if we have sufficient knowledge of the processes involved.

~ William Burroughs

Being a physician certainly doesn't make one immune to human suffering, nor should it, but one does become less vulnerable if there is happiness in one's own life.

~ Sigmund Freud

What a man knows at fifty that he did not know at twenty is for the most part incommunicable.

~ Adlai Stevenson

To blind oneself to change is not to halt it.

~ Isaac Goldberg

No life is so hard that you can't make it easier by the way you take it.

~ Ellen Glasgow

The art of writing is the art of discovering what you believe.

~ David Hare

People tend to spend their adult years either reliving or trying to terminate the image they carried in high school.

Be the change you wish to see in the world.

~ Mohandas K. Gandhi

A man must learn to forgive himself.

~ Arthur Davison Ficke

In philosophy an individual is becoming himself.

~ Bernard Lonergan

A nation without the means of reform is without the means of survival.

~ Edmund Burke

Everyone is a prisoner of his own experiences. No one can eliminate prejudices – just recognize them.

~ Edward R. Murrow

It all depends on how we look at things, not how they are in themselves.

~ Carl G. Jung

Have patience with all things, but chiefly patience with yourself. Do not lose courage in considering your own imperfections, but instantly set about remedying them – every day begin the task anew.

~ St. Francis de Sales

Sometimes a man imagines that he will lose himself if he gives himself, and keep himself if he hides himself. But the contrary takes place with terrible exactitude.

~ Ernest Hello

The art of progress is to preserve order amid change, and to preserve change amid order.

~ Alfred North Whitehead

He that will not apply new remedies must expect new evils, for time is the greatest innovator.

~ Francis Bacon

Of our conflicts with others we make rhetoric; of our conflicts with ourselves we make poetry.

~ William Butler Yeats

The happiness of a man in this life does not consist in the absence but in the mastery of his passions.

~ Alfred, Lord Tennyson

We awaken in others the same attitude of mind we hold toward them.

~ Elbert Hubbard

When one has not had a good father, one must create one.

~ Friedrich Nietzsche

There is nothing noble about being superior to some other men. The true nobility is in being superior to your previous self.

~ Hindustani proverb

Man is a complex being: he makes deserts bloom and lakes die.

~ Gil Stern

Do not be too moral. You may cheat yourself out of much life. So aim above morality. Be not simply good; be good for something.

~ Henry David Thoreau

The mother-child relationship is paradoxical and, in a sense, tragic. It requires the most intense love on the mother's side, yet this very love must help the child grow away from the mother and to become fully independent.

~ Erich Fromm

If your morals make you dreary, depend on it they are wrong.

~ Robert Louis Stevenson

What the mother sings to the cradle goes all the way down to the coffin.

~ Henry Ward Beecher

One must choose in life between boredom and suffering.

~ Madame de Stael

From error to error one discovers the entire truth.

~ Sigmund Freud

Words are the physicians of a mind diseased.

~ Aeschylus

I think that somehow, we learn who we really are and then live with that decision.

~ Eleanor Roosevelt

All men should strive to learn before they die
What they are running from, and to, and why.

~ James Thurber

The sign of an intelligent person is their ability to control emotions by the application of reason.

~ Marya Mannes

Every theory of love, from Plato down, teaches that each individual loves in the other sex what he lacks in himself.

~ G. Stanley Hall

Loneliness is and always has been the central and inevitable experience of every man.

~ Thomas Wolfe

Experience is in the fingers and the head. The heart is inexperienced.

~ Henry David Thoreau

Character building begins in our infancy, and continues until death.

~ Eleanor Roosevelt

We only become what we are by the radical and deep-seeded refusal of that which others have made of us.

~ Jean-Paul Sartre

All changes, even the most longed for, have their melancholy, for what we leave behind us is a part of ourselves; we must die to one life before we can enter into another.

~ Anatole France

All that is human must retrograde if it does not advance.

~ Edward Gibbon

It is in the nature of a man as he grows older... to protest against change, particularly change for the better.

~ John Steinbeck

When we are unable to find tranquility within ourselves, it is useless to seek it elsewhere.

~ Francois, Duc de La Rochefoucauld

Psychoanalysis is not the only way to resolve inner conflicts. Life itself still remains a very effective therapist.

~ Karen Horney

Out of my great woe
I make my little song.

~ Heinrich Heine

He knows the universe, but himself he does not know.

~ La Fontaine

Ninety-nine percent of people in the world are fools and the rest of us are in great danger of contagion.

~ Thornton Wilder

When one is a stranger to oneself then one is estranged from others too.

~ Anne Morrow Lindbergh

Space flights are merely an escape, a fleeing away from one-self, because it is easier to go to Mars or to the moon than it is to penetrate one's being.

~ Carl Jung

People often say that this or that person has not yet found himself. But the self is not something that one finds. It is something that one creates.

~ Thomas Szasz

We are healed from suffering only by experiencing it to the full.

~ Marcel Proust

Only in growth, reform, and change, paradoxically enough, is true security to be found.

~ Anne Morrow Lindbergh

Could it be that I may spend the rest of my life attempting to reconcile the ambiguities, the polar opposites that appear to be inherent in the universe, in society, in myself?

Only God and some few rare geniuses can keep forging ahead into novelty.

~ Denis Diderot

Look into the depths of your own soul and learn first to know yourself, then you will understand why this illness was bound to come upon you and perhaps you will thenceforth avoid falling ill.

~ Sigmund Freud

The methods that help a man acquire a fortune are the very ones that keep him from enjoying it.

~ Antoine de Rivarol

Every man has seen the wall that limits his mind.

~ Alfred de Vigny

A person's maturity consists in having found again the seriousness one had as a child, at play.

~ Friedrich Nietzsche

When does self-observation, self-appraisal become too much? Those inclined toward "knowing themselves" often have the idea that more analysis is better, and that in the future we will be better off because of it. I'm afraid that while others whom I call simplistic, superficial or ignorant are living life to a greater degree than I am. Essentially, am I worrying, or growing, when I work on myself?

Wisdom and virtue are like the two wheels of a cart.

~ Japanese proverb

Although the world is full of suffering, it is full also of the overcoming of it.

~ Helen Keller

[Liberalism is not...] *what* opinions are held, but... *how* they are held: instead of being held dogmatically, [liberal] opinions are held tentatively, and with a consciousness that new evidence may at any moment lead to their abandonment.

~ Bertrand Russell

People wish to be settled: only as far as they are unsettled is there any hope for them.

~ Ralph Waldo Emerson

We are what other people say we are. We know ourselves through hearsay.

~ Eric Hofer

If a man in the morning hears the right way, he may die in the evening without regret.

~ Confucius

There can be no peace of mind in love, since the advantage one has secured is never anything but a fresh starting point for further desires.

~ Marcel Proust

Aloofness does not protect one, rather, it isolates him.

The fact that conscience remains partially infantile throughout life is the core of human tragedy.

~ Erik Erikson

Diplomacy and defense are not substitutes for each other. Either alone would fail.

~ John F. Kennedy

If your goal is to avoid pain and escape suffering, I would not advise you to seek higher levels of consciousness or spiritual evolution.

~ M. Scott Peck

Carpenters fashion wood; fletchers fashion arrows; the wise fashion themselves

~ Buddha

Man is the measure of all things.

~ Protagoras

If you feel you have both feet planted on level ground, then the university has failed you.

~ Robert Goheen

The essence of being human is that one does not seek perfection.

~ George Orwell

Energy transmitted between humans and the external world,
Is similar in our minds to the figurative flag not yet unfurled.
The power of the unconscious mind is hardly recognized,
Save for Freud, the existence routinely circumscribed.

Only the mediocre are always at their best.

~ Jean Giraudoux

Change is one thing, progress is another. "Change" is scientific, "progress" is ethical; change is indisputable, whereas progress is a matter of controversy.

~ Bertrand Russell

This is not the end of the story of my life-
Oh no, my unyielding determination buoys me.
A tireless struggle to become all that I can-
The sapling that is my heart will become a tree.

Genius is formed in quiet, character in the stream of life.

~ Johann Wolfgang Goethe

As long as people will accept crap, it will be financially profitable to dispense it.

~ Dick Cavett

Communality is as honorable as individuality.
Everything is in a state of flux, including the status quo.

~ Robert Byrne

Man *becomes* man only by the intelligence, but he *is* man only by the heart.

~ Henri Frederic Amiel

How much more grievous are the consequences of anger than the causes of it!

~ Marcus Aurelius

Just as the twig is bent, the tree is inclined.

~ Alexander Pope

History teaches us that men and nations behave wisely once they have exhausted all other alternatives.

~ Abba Eban

He's got to make his own mistakes,
And learn to mend the mess he makes.
He's old enough to know what's right, but young enough not to choose it.
He's noble enough to win the world, but weak enough to lose it.

~ Neil Peart

Neurosis is always a substitute for legitimate suffering.

~ Carl Jung

Grow up, and that is a terribly hard thing to do. It is much easier to skip it and go from one childhood to another.

~ F. Scott Fitzgerald

For people with an "emotional distance/closeness" problem, there is a gross paradox; for they long for closeness until such time as they have it, and then they long for distance once again.

Blame someone else and get on with your life.

~ Alan Woods

Resentment is like drinking poison and waiting for the other person to die.

~ Carrie Fisher

For any sensible person, money is two things: a major liberating force and a great convenience. It's devastating to those who have in mind something else.

~ John Kenneth Galbraith

Everyone thinks of changing the world, but no one thinks of changing himself.

~ Leo Tolstoy

For some folks, it's not what they do for work; it's what they do when they're not working that defines their health and constitutes their challenge.

Live in such a way that you would not be ashamed to sell your parrot to the town gossip.

~ Will Rogers

Cocksure men of evil ways abuse the power they own.
Throughout the centuries it has consistently been shown
That those men of weak spirit, with dark souls depraved and impure,
Despite their years, have not grown beyond intentions immature.

Human nature is not a machine to be built after a model, and set to do exactly the work prescribed for it, but a tree, which requires to grow and develop itself on all sides, according to the tendency of the inward forces which make it a living thing.

~ John Stuart Mill

Reality is the leading cause of stress amongst those in touch with it.

~ Jane Wagner (and Lily Tomlin)

So long as men praise you, you can only be sure that you are not yet on your own path but on someone else's.

~ Friedrich Nietzsche

All the world's a stage and most of us are desperately unrehearsed.

~ Sean O'Casey

A man of active and resilient mind outwears his friendships just as certainly as he outwears his love affairs, his politics and his epistemology.

~ H. L. Mencken

Intelligence is a necessary, but not sufficient, precondition of enlightenment.

Most conversations are simply monologues delivered in the presence of witnesses.

~ Margaret Millar

The direct use of force is such a poor solution to any problem, it is generally employed only by small children and large nations.

~ David Friedman

Boys will be boys, and so will a lot of middle-aged men.

~ Kin Hubbard

The first principle is that you must not fool yourself - and you are the easiest person to fool.

~ Richard Feynman

Progress might have been all right once, but it has gone on too long.

~ Ogden Nash

Exposing our most shameful parts involves trust ~
It takes faith to allow others to peer into one's soul.
Tolerance is required when we tell our full story;
Integration is fitting the pieces into a whole.

It is easier to fight for one's principles than to live up to them.

~ Alfred Adler

To understand the heart and mind of a person, look not at what he has already achieved, but at what he aspires to do.

~ Kahlil Gibran

Use, do not abuse; neither abstinence nor excess ever renders man happy.

~ Voltaire

A talent is formed in stillness, a character in the world's torrent

~ Johann Wolfgang von Goethe

Strange how the feelings return
After years of emptiness.
Unexpectedly, the burn,
And the chill of loneliness

There are people whose watch stops at a certain hour and who remain permanently at that age.

~ Charles Augustin Sainte-Beuve

I must have been an idiot. I've become self-educated since I wrote "The Okie from Muskogee."

~ Merle Haggard

Balance is a worthy path to take.
Pursuing the highs and accepting the lows.
But time is too valuable to waste,
Because watching TV., no one ever grows.

Wise men talk because they have something to say; fools, because they have to say something.

~ Plato

My problem lies in reconciling my gross habits with my net income.

~ Errol Flynn

All the knowledge I possess everyone else can acquire, but my heart is all my own.

~ Johann Wolfgang von Goethe

Peace and love should be goals sought above all else-
Including dominance, wealth, and status in a
profession.
Size should become passé as the preeminent mark of a
man.
By growing emotionally and morally man can end his
obsessions.

The ability to delude yourself may be an important
survival tool.

~ Jane Wagner

Be careful about reading health books. You may die of
a misprint.

~ Mark Twain

The penalty for success is to be bored by the people
who used to snub you.

~ Nancy Astor

I have discovered that all human evil comes from this,
man's being unable to sit still in a room.

~ Blaise Pascal

One must *be* something to be able to *do* something.

~ Johann Wolfgang von Goethe

Experience is not what happens to a man.   It is what a man does with what happens to him.

~ Aldous Huxley

We rise in thought to the heavenly throne, but our own nature still remains unknown.

~ Voltaire

As human beings, our greatness lies not so much in being able to remake the world – that is the myth of the Atomic Age – as in being able to remake ourselves.

~ Mohandas K. Gandhi

When I feel nostalgic about the past or worried about the future, sometimes it helps to get more vigorously involved in the present moment, to work on myself, to push myself.

Little minds are tamed and subdued by misfortune; but great minds rise above them.

~ Washington Irving

After a certain age, the more one becomes oneself, the more obvious one's family traits become.

~ Marcel Proust

The important thing is not to stop questioning.

~ Albert Einstein

When you're through changing, you're through.

~ Bruce Barton

I am as lost as any philosopher or child;
Half of me wants solace, the other to be wild.

Everybody wants to be somebody: Nobody wants to grow.

~ Johann Wolfgang von Goethe

CREATIVITY, INGENUITY & VISION

An idea is a greater monument than a cathedral.

~ Clarence Darrow

Vision is the art of seeing things invisible.

~ Jonathan Swift

Almost everything that is great has been done by youth.

~ Benjamin Disraeli

Clown and guru are a single identity: the satiric and sublime side of the same higher vision of life.

~ Theodore Rozak

Happiness lies in the joy of achievement and the thrill of creative effort.

~ Franklin D. Roosevelt

It is discouraging to try to penetrate a mind like yours. You ought to get it out and dance on it. That would take some of the rigidity out of it.

~ Mark Twain

Light comes to us unexpectedly and obliquely. Perhaps it amuses the gods to try us. They want to see whether we are asleep.

~ H. M. Tomlinson

A conservative believes nothing should be done for the first time.

~ Lynwood L. Giacomini

The decline of literature indicates the decline of a nation.

~ Johann Wolfgang von Goethe

Science is for those who learn; poetry for those who know.

~ Joseph Roux

Writing free verse is like playing tennis with the net down.

~ Robert Frost

Discovery consists of seeing what everybody has seen and thinking what nobody has thought.

~ Albert von Szent-Gyorgyi

I like to think of thoughts as living blossoms borne by the human tree.

~ James Douglas

The true poet is all the time a visionary and whether with friends or not, as much alone as a man on his death bed.

~ W. B. Yeats

The genius of Einstein leads to Hiroshima.

~ Pablo Picasso

Half the pleasure of life consists of the opportunities one has neglected.

~ Oliver W. Holmes, Jr.

A clown is a poet in action.

~ Henry Miller

A poem is never finished, only abandoned.

~ Paul Valery

The height of cleverness is to be able to conceal it.

~ Francois, Duc de La Rochefoucauld

Life is so largely controlled by chance that its conduct can be but a perpetual improvisation.

~ W. Somerset Maugham

No one sees further into a generalization than his own knowledge of the details extends.

~ William James

We must be willing to get rid of the life we've planned, so as to have the life that is awaiting us... The old skin has to be shed before the new one is to come.

~ Joseph Campbell

There is a great deal of self-will in the world, but very little genuine independence of character.

~ Frederick W. Faber

Very simple ideas are within the reach of only very complicated minds.

~ Remy de Gourmont

You've got to do your own growing, no matter how tall your grandfather was.

~ Irish proverb

Fear is the static that prevents me from hearing my intuition.

~ Hugh Prather

The beautiful feeling after writing a poem is on the whole better even than after sex, and that's saying a lot.

~ Anne Sexton

Colleges hate geniuses, just as convents hate saints.

~ Ralph Waldo Emerson

I'm nobody's steady date. I can always be distracted by love, but eventually I get horny for my creativity.

~ Gilda Radner

The very essence of the creative is its novelty, and hence we have no standard by which to judge it.

~ Carl Rogers

To live remains an art which everyone must learn and which no one can teach.

~ Havelock Ellis

I lived in solitude in the country and noticed how the monotony of a quiet life stimulates the creative mind.

~ Albert Einstein

I know of no more encouraging fact than the unquestionable ability of man to elevate his life by a conscious endeavor.

~ Henry David Thoreau

I am always doing that which I can not do, in order that I may learn how to do it.

~ Pablo Picasso

An invasion of armies can be resisted, but not an idea whose time has come.

~ Victor Hugo

One machine can do the work of fifty ordinary men. No machine can do the work of one extraordinary man.

~ Elbert Hubbard

We take our shape, it is true, within and against that cage of reality bequeathed us at our birth, and yet it is precisely through our dependence on this reality that we are most endlessly betrayed.

~ James Baldwin

The main obligation is to amuse yourself.

~ S. J. Perelman

A man is not idle because he is absorbed in thought. There is a visible labour and there is an invisible labour.

~ Victor Hugo

I do not feel obliged to believe that the same God who has endowed us with sense, reason, and intellect has intended us to forgo their use.

~ Galileo Galilei

I quote others in order to better express my own self.

~ Michel de Montaigne

It distresses me, this failure to keep pace with the leaders of thought, as they pass in to oblivion.

~ Max Beerbohm

Riches enlarge, rather than satisfy appetites.

~ Thomas Fuller

It wasn't raining when Noah built the ark.

~ Howard Ruff

A man is not old until regrets take the place of dreams.

~ John Barrymore

To see what is in front of one's nose needs a constant struggle.

~ George Orwell

Daring ideas are like chessmen moved forward. They may be beaten, but they may start a winning game.

~ Johann Wolfgang von Goethe

The world owes all its onward impulses to men ill at ease. The happy man inevitably confines himself within ancient limits.

~ Nathaniel Hawthorne

Let early education be a sort of amusement; you will be then be better able to find out the natural bent.

~ Plato

Color, which is the poet's wealth, is so expensive that most take to mere outline sketches and become men of science.

~ Henry David Thoreau

The free man is he who does not fear to go to the end of his thought.

~ Leon Blum

When a poet's mind is perfectly equipped for its work, it is constantly amalgamating disparate experiences.

~ T. S. Eliot

I have learned to use the word 'impossible' with the greatest caution.

~ Wernher von Braun

One's task is not to turn the world upside down, but to do what is necessary at the given place and with a due consideration of reality.

~ Dietrich Bonhoeffer

I passionately hate the idea of being with it, I think an artist has always to be out of step with his time.

~ Orson Welles

Don't limit your child to your own learning, for he was born in another time.

~ Rabbinical saying

Originality is nothing but judicious imitation.

~ Voltaire

Pessimist- one who, when he has the choice of two evils, chooses both.

~ Oscar Wilde

Creativity requires the freedom to consider "unthinkable" alternatives, to doubt the worth of cherished practices.

~ John W. Gardner

Our unconsciousness is like a vast subterranean factory with intricate machinery that is never idle, where work goes on day and night from the time we are born until the moment of our death.

~ Milton R. Sapirstein

Curiosity is a lust of the mind.

~ Thomas Hobbes

Let us not forget that the greatest composers were also the greatest thieves. They stole from everyone and everywhere.

~ Pablo Casals

Common sense is the collection of prejudices acquired by age 18.

~ Albert Einstein

Music is a strange thing. I would say it is a miracle. For it stands halfway between thought and phenomenon, between spirit and matter.

~ Heinrich Heine

The irony of love is that it guarantees some degree of anger, fear and criticism.

~ Harold H. Bloomfield

When love and skill work together, expect a masterpiece.

~ John Ruskin

As a man is, so he sees.

~ William Blake

Living consciously is not out of our grasp. It does not mean living a life of Gandhi or the Dalai Lama. Imagine how the world would be if we just made a few simple changes within ourselves. Recycle used packages. Shop at responsible food sellers. See where that garment was made before selecting it. Read about the world. Vote informed. Continue to become more educated. Say hello to your neighbor and stay out of their business when it does not directly impact your comfort. Have an occupation that pleases you and doesn't exploit others. Choose a car that is reasonably fuel-efficient. We must then face the frustration of watching the ignorant person throw trash out their car window, or that some corporations are swamping our little acts of responsibility. But that's okay. We really are only responsible for certain things, and others really are out of our control. But recall with imagination the fact that if we each do our own little part, then the world is changed.

You cannot put a rope around the neck of an idea: you cannot put an idea up against a barrack-square wall and riddle it with bullets: you cannot confine it in the strongest prison cell that your slaves could ever build.

~ Sean O'Casey

Why is this thus? What is the reason for this thusness?

~ Artemus Ward

A proverb is no proverb to you until life has illustrated it.

~ John Keats

My body has certainly wandered a good deal, but I have an uneasy suspicion that my mind has not wandered enough.

~ Noel Coward

In Chinese, the word for crisis is wei ji, composed of the character wei, which means danger, and ji, which means opportunity.

~ Jan Wong

A man is not necessarily intelligent because he has plenty of ideas, any more than he is a good general because he has plenty of soldiers.

~ Sebastien Chamfort

The eyes are not responsible when the mind does the seeing.

~ Publilius Syrus

Inspiration could be called inhaling the memory of an act never experienced.

~ Ned Rorem

When one door of happiness closes, another opens; but often we look so long at the closed door that we do not see the one which has been opened for us.

~ Helen Keller

The job of intellectuals is to come up with ideas, and all we've been producing is footnotes.

~ Theodore White

Madness is to think of too many things in succession too fast, or of one thing too exclusively.

~ Voltaire

The creation of a thousand forests is in one acorn.

~ Ralph Waldo Emerson

Anyone who lives within his means suffers from a lack of imagination.

~ Lionel Stander

The great thing in this world is not so much where we stand, as in what direction we are moving.

~ Oliver Wendell Holmes

Every man takes the limits of his own field of vision for the limits of the world.

~ Arthur Schopenhauer

The fellow that can only see a week ahead is always the popular fellow, for he is looking with the crowd. But the one that can see years ahead, he has a telescope but he can't make anybody believe he has it.

~ Mark Twain

An intellectual is someone whose mind watches itself.

~ Albert Camus

Poetry is the language in which man explores his own amazement.

~ Christopher Fry

If we must accept Fate, we are no less compelled to affirm liberty, the significance of the individual, the grandeur of duty, the power of character.

~ Ralph Waldo Emerson

A rock pile ceases to be a rock pile the moment a single man contemplates it, bearing within him the image of a cathedral.

~ Antoine de Saint-Exupery

The man who, in a fit of melancholy, kills himself today, would have wished to live if he'd waited a week.

~ Voltaire

What is the hardest task in the world? To think.

~ Ralph Waldo Emerson

There is but one success - to be able to spend your life in your own way.

~ Christopher Morley

Everyone has a talent; what is rare is the courage to follow the talent to the dark place where it leads.

~ Erica Jong

Intellectually, religious emotions are not creative but conservative. They attach themselves readily to the current view of the world and consecrate it.

~ John Dewey

The eager and often inconsiderate appeals of reformers and revolutionists are indispensable to counterbalance the inertia and fossilism marking so large a part of human institutions.

~ Walt Whitman

The art of creation is older than the art of killing.

~ Andrei Voznesensky

I prefer the company of peasants because they have not been educated sufficiently to reason incorrectly.

~ Michel de Montaigne

Comic vision leads to serious solutions.

~ Malcolm L. Kushner

Let us leave every man free to search within himself and lose himself in his ideas.

~ Voltaire

If they give you ruled paper, write the other way.

~ Juan Ramon Jiminez

The devil does not stay where music is.

~ Martin Luther

The works of great poets have never yet been read by mankind, for only great poets can read them.

~ Henry David Thoreau

What is so wonderful about literature is that it transforms the man who reads it towards the condition of the man who wrote.

~ E. M. Forster

It is probable that democracy owes more to nonconformity that any other single movement.

~ R. H. Tawney

I know of no country in which there is so little independence of mind...as in America.

~ Alexis de Tocqueville

Iron rusts from disuse, stagnant water loses its purity and in cold weather becomes frozen; even so does inaction sap the vigor of the mind.

~ Leonardo da Vinci

To be a wit, intelligence is enough. To be a poet takes imagination.

~ Cardinal de Bernis

One often makes a remark and only later sees how true it is.

~ Ludwig Wittgenstein

A wise man will make more opportunities than he finds.

~ Francis Bacon

It were not best that we should think alike; it is difference of opinion that makes horse races.

~ Mark Twain

The vast majority of human beings dislike and even actually dread all notions with which they are not familiar...hence innovators have generally been persecuted and always derided as fools and madmen.

~ Aldous Huxley

Every man takes the limits of his own field of vision for the limits of the world.

~ Arthur Schopenhauer

The worst pain we can have is to know much as be impotent to act.

~ Herodotus

Heard melodies are sweet, but those unheard are sweeter.

~ John Keats

Man cannot overestimate the greatness and power of his mind.

~ George Frederick Hegel

Genius means little more than the faculty of perceiving in an unhabitual way.

~ William James

The gift of fantasy has meant more to me than my talent for absorbing positive knowledge.

~ Albert Einstein

Every great advance in natural knowledge has involved the absolute rejection of authority.

~ T. H. Huxley

When a nation's young men are conservative, its funeral bell is already rung.

~ Henry Ward Beecher

I can't understand why people are frightened by new ideas. I'm frightened by the old ones.

~ John Cage

Fanaticism consists in redoubling your efforts when you have forgotten your aim.

~ George Santyana

...there is a natural aristocracy among men. The grounds of this are virtue and talent.

~ Thomas Jefferson

A reactionary is someone with a clear and comprehensive vision of an ideal world we have lost.

~ Kenneth Minogue

Literature is the human activity that takes the fullest and most precise account of variousness, possibility, complexity, and difficulty.

~ Lionel Trilling

Why accept darkness over seeing,
When the light can actually be lit?
The funny thing about smog being,
Over time, you fail to notice it.

Longfellow serenade, such were the plans I'd made, For she was a lady, and I was a dreamer, with only words to trade....

~ Neil Diamond

You can't make up anything anymore. The world itself is a satire. All you're doing is recording it.

~ Art Buchwald

Love looks not with the eyes but with the mind.

~ William Shakespeare

There is nothing more dreadful than imagination without taste.

~ Johann Wolfgang von Goethe

The significant problems we have cannot be solved at the same level of thinking with which we created them.

~ Albert Einstein

Billions of possibilities regarding my evolution-
Thousands of seemingly random choices made.
Incalculable problems and moments with more than one solution-
Fleeting acts become permanently engraved.

A good novel tells us the truth about its hero; but a bad novel tells us the truth about its author.

~ G. K. Chesterton

Thought is the labor of the intellect, reverie its pleasure.

~ Victor Hugo

If two men agree on everything, you may be sure that one of them is doing the thinking.

~ Lyndon B. Johnson

I have learned to use the word 'impossible' with the greatest caution.

~ Wernher von Braun

Neither intelligence nor judgment are creative. If a sculptor is nothing but science and intelligence, his hands will have no talent.

~ Antoine de Saint-Exupery

After silence, that which comes nearest to expressing the inexpressible is music.

~ Aldous Huxley

When ideas fail, words come in very handy.

~ Johann Wolfgang von Goethe

There is no more ineffective method of leading human beings than the use of irritation and anger.

~ James Dobson

Logic is like the sword: those who appeal to it shall perish by it.

~ Samuel Butler

There are moments in history when the fabric of everyday life unravels, and there is this unstable dynamism that allows for incredible social change in short periods of time. People and the world they're living in can be utterly transformed, either for the good or the bad, or some mixture of the two.

~ Tony Kushner

Vision without action is a daydream. Action without vision is a nightmare.

~ Japanese proverb

Martyrdom is the only way a person can become famous without ability.

~ George Bernard Shaw

I thoroughly disapprove of duels. If a man should challenge me, I would take him kindly and forgivingly by the hand and lead him to a quiet place and kill him.

~ Mark Twain

There is no theory. You have only to listen. Pleasure is the law.

~ Claude Debussy

The surest way to corrupt a youth is to instruct him to hold in higher esteem those who think alike than those who think differently.

~ Mohandas K. Gandhi

There is no great genius without some touch of madness.

~ Lucius Annaeus Seneca

We draw our own designs; fortune has to make that frame. We come into the world and take our chances. Fate is just the weight of circumstances - Roll the Bones!

~ Neil Peart

You can't build a reputation on what you are going to do.

~ Henry Ford

We are continually faced with a series of great opportunities brilliantly disguised as insoluble problems.

~ John W. Gardner

Music is as prestigious as mathematics.

Every gun that is made, every warship launched, every rocket fired signifies a theft from those who hunger and are not fed, those who are cold and are not clothed. This world in arms is not spending money alone. It is spending the sweat of its laborers, the genius of its scientists, the hope of its children.

~ Dwight Eisenhower

Almost all new ideas have a certain aspect of foolishness when they are first produced.

~ Alfred North Whitehead

If the only tool you have is a hammer, you tend to see every problem as a nail.

~ Abraham Maslow

America must finish what we started in the Declaration of Independence and the Constitution and go all the way until we assure liberty and justice for the millions of children of all races and incomes left behind in our society today despite national leaders who seek to turn us back to the not-so-good old days of race and class and gender divisions.

~Marian Wright Edelman

Skill without imagination is craftsmanship and gives us many useful objects such as wickerwork picnic baskets. Imagination without skill gives us modern art.

~ Tom Stoppard

There is no finer investment for any country that putting milk into babies.

~ Winston Churchill

If you believe everything you read, better not read.

~ Japanese Proverb

The man of faith, the believer, is necessarily a small type of man. Hence, 'freedom of spirit' i.e., *unbelief*, as an instinct is a precondition of greatness.

~ Friedrich Nietzsche

It is a spiritually impoverished nation that permits infants and children to be the poorest Americans.

~ Marian Wright Edelman

Dictionary definition of parallax: "apparent change in the position of an object resulting from the change in the direction or position from which it is viewed."

Art is making something out of nothing and selling it.

~ Frank Zappa

We know too much and feel too little. At least, we feel too little of those creative emotions from which a good life springs.

~ Bertrand Russell

Imagination is the one weapon in the war against reality.

~ Jules de Gaultier

Every phenomenon, every object, can be observed in alternative ways. You can disperse that mind-altering haze, and yet the noumenon remains unchanged.
Some things have to be believed to be seen.

~ Ralph Hodgson

Intellect annuls fate: So far as a man thinks, he is free.

~ Ralph Waldo Emerson

A poet looks at the world the way a man looks at a woman.

~ Wallace Stevens

Every man who knows how to read has it in his power to magnify himself, to multiply the ways in which he exists, to make his life full, significant and interesting.

~ Aldous Huxley

They are able because they think they are able.

~ Virgil

The whole problem can be stated quite simply by asking, 'Is there a meaning to music?' My answer would be, 'Yes.' And 'Can you state in so many words what the meaning is?' My answer to that would be, 'No.'

~ Aaron Copland

It is a far, far better thing to have a firm anchor in nonsense than to put out on the troubled sea of thought.

~ John Kenneth Galbraith

Research is the process of going up alleys to see if they are blind.

~ Marston Bates

All generalizations are dangerous, even this one.

~ Alexandre Dumas

If an elderly but distinguished scientist says that something is possible he is almost certainly right, but if he says that it is impossible he is very probably wrong.

~ Arthur C. Clarke

Discovery consists of seeing what everybody sees and thinking what nobody has thought.

~ Albert von Szent-Gyorgyi

A paranoid is someone who knows a little of what's going on.

~ William Burroughs

Love thy neighbour as yourself, but choose your neighbourhood.

~ Louise Beal

Tradition is what you resort to when you don't have the time or the money to do it right.

~ Kurt Herbert Alder

At my lemonade stand I used to give the first glass away free and charge five dollars for the second glass. The refill contained the antidote.

~ Emo Phillips

Human salvation lies in the hands of the creatively maladjusted.

~ Martin Luther King, Jr.

The only way to discover the limits of the possible is to go beyond them into the impossible.

~ Arthur C. Clarke

If we don't change direction soon, we'll end up where we're going.

~ Irwin Corey

Whatever you may be sure of, be sure of this: That you are dreadfully like other people.

~ James Russell Lowell

Let early education be a sort of amusement; you will then be better able to discover the [child's] natural bent.

~ Plato

For every human problem, there is a neat, simple solution; and it is always wrong

~ H. L. Mencken

Nothing is more conducive to peace of mind than not having any opinions at all.

~ Georg Christoph Lichtenberg

The most beautiful thing we can experience is the mysterious. It is the source of all true art and science.

~ Albert Einstein

How many people become abstract as a way of appearing profound!

~ Joseph Joubert

If Columbus had an advisory committee, he would probably still be at the dock.

~ Arthur Goldberg

Great geniuses have the shortest biographies: Their cousins can tell you nothing about them.

~ Ralph Waldo Emerson

In creating, the only hard thing's to begin; a grass-blade's no easier to make than an oak.

~ James Russell Lowell

A great flame follows a little spark.

~ Dante Aligheri

Men have become the tools of their tools.

~ Henry David Thoreau

KNOWLEDGE, WISDOM & EDUCATION

To know that we know what we know, and that we do not know what we do not know, that is true knowledge.

~ Henry David Thoreau

How freely we live life depends both on our political system and on our vigilance in defending its liberties. How long we live depends both on our genes and on the quality of our health care. How well we live ~ that is, how thoughtfully, how nobly, how virtuously, how joyously, how lovingly – depends both on our philosophy and on the way we apply it to all else. The examined life is a better life...

~ Lou Marinoff

Belief is harder to shake than knowledge.

~ Adolf Hitler

Profundity of thought belongs to youth, clarity of thought to old age.

~ Friedrich Nietzsche

Aristotle was famous for knowing everything. He taught that the brain exists merely to cool the blood and is not involved in the process of thinking. This is true only of certain persons.

~ Will Cuppy

The most certain way to hide from others the limits of our knowledge is not to go beyond them.

~ Giacomo Leopardi

I am not quite sure what the advantage is in having a few more dollars to spend if the air is too dirty to breathe, the water too polluted to drink, the commuters are losing in the struggle to get in and out of the city, the streets are filthy, the schools so bad that the young perhaps wisely stay away, and the hoodlums roll citizens for some of the dollars they saved in the tax cut.

~ John Kenneth Galbraith

The intellect is always fooled by the heart.

~ Francois, Duc de La Rochefoucauld

The only means of strengthening one's intellect is to make up one's mind about nothing – to let the mind be a thoroughfare for all thoughts.

~ John Keats

The more one penetrates the realm of knowledge the more puzzling everything becomes.

~ Henry Miller

To be conscious that you are ignorant is a great step toward knowledge.

~ Benjamin Disraeli

Philosophy will clip an angel's wings,
Conquer all mysteries by rule and line,
Empty the haunted air, and gnomed mine-
Unweave a rainbow.

~ John Keats

The last function of reason is to recognize that there is an infinity of things which surpass it.

~ Blaise Pascal

[Let us oppose] one species of superstition to another, set them a-quarreling; while we ourselves...happily make our escape into the calm, though obscure, regions of philosophy.

~ David Hume

Religion is the masterpiece of the art of animal training, for it trains people as to how they shall think.

~ Arthur Schopenhauer

We live in an era and a time where calling someone an Einstein is considered to be somewhat of an insult! Morons are out there in force-- making left-hand turns from right-hand lanes, trying to pay for drive-thru tacos with a fucking check, calling 411 to get the number for information.... What happened? First and foremost, as a matter of fact, numbers 1, 2, and ... what comes after 2?... we didn't pay enough attention to our education system.

~ Dennis Miller

Prejudice is never easy unless it can pass itself off for reason.

~ William Hazlitt

The man who lives free from folly is not so wise as he thinks.

~ Francois, Duc de La Rochefoucauld

Men are idolaters, and want something to look at and kiss and hug, or throw themselves down before; they always did, they always will, and if you don't make it out of wood, you must make it out of words.

~ Oliver Wendell Holmes

Why is it necessary to fall down a manhole to find out that it's a bad idea?

~ Murray Bowen

Thought is great and swift and free, the light of the world, and the chief glory of man.

~ Bertrand Russell

It is so important for the purpose of thought to keep language efficient as it is in surgery to keep *tetanus bacilli* out of one's bandages.

~ Ezra Pound

To be able to ask a question is clearly two-thirds of the way to getting it answered.

~ John Ruskin

If you want to understand today, you have to search yesterday.

~ Pearl Buck

If we would have new knowledge, we must get a whole world of new questions.

~ Susanne K. Langer

A great memory is never made synonymous with wisdom, any more than a dictionary would be called a treatise.

~ John H. Cardinal Newman

Fools rush in where angels fear to tread.

~ Alexander Pope

Philosophy – the purple bullfinch in the lilac tree.

~ T. S. Eliot

A wise man proportions his belief to the evidence.

~ Immanuel Kant

From listening comes wisdom, and from speaking, repentance.

~ Italian proverb

I respect faith, but doubt is what gets you an education.

~ Wilson Mizner

He has a first-rate mind until he makes it up.

~ Violet Bonham Carter

A good listener is not only popular everywhere, but after a while he gets to know something.

~ Wilson Mizner

Men give me credit for genius; but all the genius I have lies in this: When I have a subject on hand I study it profoundly.

~ Alexander Hamilton

The average man's judgment is so poor, he runs a risk every time he uses it.

~ E. W. Howe

I have steadily endeavored to keep my mind free so as to give up any hypothesis, however much beloved... as soon as facts are shown to be opposed to it.

~ Charles Darwin

To be ignorant of one's ignorance is the malady of ignorance.

~ A. Bronson Alcott

Knowledge rests not upon truth alone, but upon error also.

~ Carl Jung

One of the greatest pains to human nature is the pain of a new idea.

~ Walter Bagehot

Socrates, the Athenian gadfly, transformed casual conversations into full-blown quests for philosophical truth.

~ Jon Spayde

As the water shapes itself to the vessel that contains it, so a wise man adapts himself to circumstances.

~ Confucius

In these matters the only certainty is that there is nothing for certain.

~ Pliny the Elder

The trouble with the world is that the stupid are cocksure and the intelligent are full of doubt.

~ Bertrand Russell

Our dignity is not in what we do, but what we understand. The whole world is doing things.

~ George Santyana

Almost all important questions are important precisely because they are not susceptible to quantitative answer.

~ Arthur Schlesinger, Jr.

The last advance of reason is to recognize that it is surpassed by innumerable things; it is feeble if it cannot realize that.

~ Blaise Pascal

Give a man a fish and you feed him for a day. Teach a man to fish and you feed him for a lifetime.

~ Chinese proverb

I have never seen a greater monster or miracle in the world than myself.

~ Michel de Montaigne

The roots of education are bitter, but the fruits are sweet.

~ Aristotle

Silence is as full of potential wisdom and wit as the unhewn marble of great sculpture.

~ Aldous Huxley

The mind of a bigot is like the pupil of the eye; the more light you pour upon it, the more it will contract.

~ Oliver Wendell Holmes, Jr.

Science is the attempt to make the chaotic diversity of our sense-experience correspond to a logically uniform system of thought.

~ Albert Einstein

You live and learn. At any rate, you live.

~ Douglas Adams

A library is thought in cold storage.

~ Herbert Samuel

Wisdom is always an overmatch for strength.

~ Phaedrus

Nothing that is worth knowing can be taught.

~ Oscar Wilde

What is research, but a blind date with knowledge?

~ Will Henry

The only thing we learn from history is that we do not learn.

~ Earl Warren

Once learning is solidified, all is over with it.

~ Alfred North Whitehead

How can I know what I think 'till I see what I say?

~ E. M. Forster

Knowledge can be communicated, but not wisdom.

~ Hermann Hesse

Only the shallow know themselves.

~ Oscar Wilde

Prejudice is the child of ignorance.

~ William Hazlitt

Education is the ability to listen to almost anything without losing your temper.

~ Robert Frost

Poverty makes you sad as well as wise.

~ Bertolt Brecht

Philosophy is a good horse in the stable, but an errant jade on a journey.

~ Oliver Goldsmith

To teach how to live with uncertainty, and yet without being paralyzed by hesitation is perhaps the chief thing that philosophy in our age can still do for those who study it.

~ Bertrand Russell

Too often we...enjoy the comfort of opinion without the discomfort of thought.

~ John F. Kennedy

People don't ask for facts in making up their minds. They would rather have one good, soul-satisfying emotion than a dozen facts.

~ Robert Keith Leavitt

Never cut what you can untie.

~ Joseph Joubert

It is better to hear the rebuke of the wise than for a man to hear the song of fools.

~ Ecclesiastes

Life would be infinitely happier if we could only be born at the age of eighty and gradually approach eighteen.

~ Mark Twain

A good mind possesses a kingdom: a great fortune is a great slavery.

~ Lucius Annaeus Seneca

It is in fact a part of the function of education to help us to escape, not from our own time – for we are bound by that – but from the intellectual and emotional limitations of our time.

~ T. S. Eliot

If you keep your mind sufficiently open, people with throw a lot of rubbish into it.

~ William A. Orton

Many a man in love with a dimple makes the mistake of marrying the whole girl.

~ Stephen Leacock

Life can only be understood backwards; but it must be lived forwards.

~ Arthur Schopenhauer

We don't know a millionth of one percent about anything.

~ Thomas A. Edison

I do not pretend to know what many ignorant men are sure of.

~ Clarence Darrow

If a little knowledge is dangerous – where is the man who has so much as to be out of danger?

~ Thomas Huxley

As we acquire more knowledge, things do not become more comprehensible, but more mysterious.

~ Albert Schweitzer

The things taught in school are not an education but the means of an education.

~ Ralph Waldo Emerson

Fools act on imagination without knowledge, pedants act on knowledge without imagination.

~ Alfred North Whitehead

We're drowning in information and starving for knowledge.

~ Rutherford D. Rogers

I have tried to know absolutely nothing about a great many things, and I have succeeded fairly well.

~ Robert Benchley

One of the functions of intelligence is to take account of the dangers that come from trusting solely to the intelligence.

~ Lewis Mumford

There is an inevitable divergence, attributed to the imperfections of the human mind, between the world as it is and the world as men perceive it.

~ James W. Fulbright

We do not receive wisdom, we have to discover it for ourselves by a voyage that no one can take for us...a voyage that no one can spare us.

~ Marcel Proust

The eyes indicate the antiquity of the soul.

~ Ralph Waldo Emerson

They know enough who know how to learn.

~ Henry Adams

We judge of man's wisdom by his hope.

~ Ralph Waldo Emerson

Let my heart be wise. It is the gods' best gift.

~ Euripides

It is good to know the truth, but better to speak of palm trees.

~ Arabic proverb

If you think education is expensive – try ignorance.

~ Derek Bok

A good education should leave much to be desired.

~ Alan Gregg

A conclusion is the place where you got tired of thinking.

~ Arthur Bloch

Learning makes a man fit company for himself.

~ Thomas Fuller

Knowledge cannot defile, nor consequently books, if the will and conscience are not defiled.

~ John Milton

Skepticism is more easily understood by asking "What do I <u>know</u>?"

~ Michel de Montaigne

Anyone who has looked deeply into the world may guess how much wisdom lies in the superficiality of men. The instinct that preserves them teaches them to be flighty, light, and false.

~ Friedrich Nietzsche

The price of wisdom is above rubies.

~ Job 28:18

Riches serve a wise man but command a fool.

~ English proverb

'Tis very puzzling on the brink
Of what is called Eternity to stare,
And know no more of what is *here*, than *there*.

~ Lord Byron

In the case of great books, the point is not to see how many of them you can get through, but rather how many can get through to you.

~ Mortimer J. Adler

The improver of knowledge absolutely refuses to acknowledge authority, as such. For him, skepticism is the highest of duties, blind faith the one unpardonable sin.

~ T. H. Huxley

You have to study a great deal to know a little.

~ Baron de Montesquieu

Our most important thoughts are those which contradict our emotions.

~ Paul Valery

What is strength without a double share of wisdom?

~ John Milton

It is dangerous to be sincere unless you are also stupid.

~ G. B. Shaw

To one without faith, no explanation is necessary. To one without faith, no explanation is possible.

~ St. Thomas Aquinas

Nothing is more terrible than ignorance in action.

~ Johann Wolfgang von Goethe

The first key to wisdom is this – constant and frequent questioning...for by doubting we are led to question and by questioning we arrive at the truth.

~ Peter Abelard

Knowledge humanizes mankind, and reason inclines to mildness; but prejudices destroy every tender disposition.

~ Baron de Montesquieu

A true philosopher is like an elephant: he never puts the second down until the first one is solidly in place.

~ Fontenelle

One may understand the cosmos, but never the ego; the self is more distant than any star.

~ G. K. Chesterton

There is no sin but ignorance.

~ Christopher Marlowe

Egotism is the anesthetic that dulls the pain of stupidity.

~ Frank Leahy

He who only knows his own side of the case, knows little of that.

~ John Stuart Mill

Just as eating against one's will is injurious to health, so study without a liking for it spoils the memory, and it retains nothing it takes in.

~ Leonardo da Vinci

He who knows others is learned; He who knows himself is wise.

~ Lao-Tzu

If any man among you seemeth to be wise in this world, let him become a fool, that he may be wise.

~ Corinthians I 3:18

If there is such a thing at all as instruction in philosophy, it can only be instruction in doing one's own thinking.

~ Leonard Nelson

When you have found out the prevailing passion of any man, remember never to trust him where that passion is concerned.

~ Lord Chesterfield

Life is a festival only to the wise.

~ Ralph Waldo Emerson

A wise man hears one word but understands two.

~ Jewish proverb

The chief characteristics of the [liberal] attitude are human sympathy, a receptivity to change, and a scientific willingness to follow reason rather than faith.

~ Chester Bowles

Certitude is not the test of certainty. We have been cocksure of many things that were not so.

~ Oliver Wendell Holmes, Jr.

That which enters the mind through reason can be corrected. That which is admitted through faith, hardly ever.

~ Santiago Ramon y Cajal

To do nothing is the most difficult thing in the world – the most difficult and the most intellectual.

~ Oscar Wilde

We cannot freely and wisely choose the right way for ourselves unless we know both good and evil.

~ Helen Keller

What is the first business of philosophy? To part with self-conceit. For it is impossible for anyone to begin to learn what he thinks he already knows.

~ Epictetus

Ignorance is not bliss – it is oblivion.

~ Philip Wylie

Cogitation & contemplation -- not indoctrination -- begets emancipation & elucidation.

To believe everything is to be an imbecile. To deny everything is to be a fool.

~ Charles Nodier

A wise man's questions contain half the answer.

~ Gabriol

Education has produced a vast population able to read but unable to distinguish was is worth reading.

~ G. M. Trevelyan

Reason is the greatest enemy faith has.

~ Martin Luther

Wherever they burn books, they will also, in the end, burn human beings.

~ Heinrich Heine

The time of human life is but a point, and the substance is a flux, and its perceptions dull, and the composition of the body corruptible, and the soul a whirl, and fortune inscrutable, and fame a senseless thing.... What then is there which can guide a man? One thing and only one, philosophy.

~ Marcus Aurelius

Only the shallow know themselves.

~ Oscar Wilde

Superstition, ignorance, supposition, and guess
Account for humans seeing dark shadows move.
Science, rationality, and logic serve us best:
Certain evil is impossible to prove.

The certainties of one age are the problems of the next.

~ R. H. Tawney

Reading furnishes the mind only with materials of knowledge; it is thinking that makes what we read ours.

~ John Locke

It is Reason alone which makes life happy and pleasant, by expelling all false conceptions or opinions....

~ Epicurus

It's bad taste to be wise all the time, like being at a perpetual funeral.

~ D. H. Lawrence

It is a characteristic of wisdom not to do desperate things.

~ Henry David Thoreau

All truths are easy to understand once they are discovered; the point is to discover them.

~ Galileo Galilei

It is possible to store the mind with a million facts and still be entirely uneducated.

~ Alec Bourne

With most men, unbelief in one thing springs from blind belief in another.

~ Georg Christoph Lichtenberg

Wisdom is a very elusive thing. Someone told me once that we often have the experience but miss the wisdom. Wisdom comes, if at all, slowly, painfully, and only after deep reflection.

~ Bill Moyers

One of the lessons of history is that nothing is often a good thing to do and always a clever thing to say.

~ Will Durant

What good fortune for those in power that people do not think.

~ Adolf Hitler

Of all the pursuits open to men, the search for wisdom is more perfect, more sublime, more profitable, and more full of joy.

~ Thomas Aquinas

A wise man sees as much as he ought, not as much as he can.

~ Michel de Montaigne

There's only one way to have a happy marriage, and as soon as I learn what it is I'll get married again.

~ Clint Eastwood

Never attribute to malice what can be adequately explained by stupidity.

~ Nick Diamos

We can be absolutely certain only about things we do not understand.

~ Eric Hoffer

Skepticism is the chastity of the intellect, and it is shameful to surrender it too soon or to the first comer.

~ George Santyana

Believe those who are seeking the truth. Doubt those who find it.

~ Andre Gide

Genius may have its limitations, but stupidity is not thus handicapped.

~ Elbert Hubbard

The man who doesn't read good books has no advantage over the man who can't read them.

~ Mark Twain

It is the mark of an educated mind to be able to entertain a thought without accepting it.

~ Aristotle

The only reason some people get lost in thought is because it's unfamiliar territory.

~ Paul Fix

Education is a state-controlled manufactory of echoes.

~ Norman Douglas

Education is the taming or domestication of the soul's raw passions – not suppressing them or excising them, which would deprive the soul of its energy – but forming and informing them as art.

~ Allan Bloom

Never try to tell everything you know. It may take too short a time.

~ Norman Ford

Understanding the atom is a childish game in comparison with the understanding of the childish game.

~ Albert Einstein

Education is a progressive discovery of our own ignorance.

~ Will Durant

Education is an admirable thing, but it is well to remember from time to time that nothing worth knowing can be taught.

~ Oscar Wilde

Youth would be an ideal state if it came a little later in life.

~ Herbert Henry Asquith

The power of accurate observation is commonly called cynicism by those who have not got it.

~ George Bernard Shaw

The older I grow, the more I distrust the familiar doctrine that age brings wisdom.

~ H. L. Mencken

Facts are stupid things.

~ Ronald Reagan

Since we cannot know all that there is to be known about anything, we ought to know a little about everything.

~ Blaise Pascal

There is no teacher who can teach us anything new. He can just help us to learn the things we always knew.

~ Michael Cretu

Argue for your limitations and sure enough, they're yours.

~ Richard Bach

It has been said that man is a rational animal. All my life I have been searching for evidence which could support this.

~ Bertrand Russell

The wise person questions himself, the fool others.

~ Henri Arnold

Doubt is not a pleasant condition but certainty is an absurd one.

~ Voltaire

Against logic there is no armor like ignorance.

~ Laurence J. Peter

We need a president who's fluent in at least one language.

~ Buck Henry

Think freely and independently or you are a slave bound by imaginary shackles. These shackles may be wrought by tradition, emotion, neediness, or fear.

Only the educated are free.

~ Epictetus

Education's purpose is to replace an empty mind with an open one.

~ Malcolm Forbes

No man's knowledge here can go beyond his experience.

~ John Locke

Computers are useless. They can only give you answers.

~ Pablo Picasso

The aim of college, for the individual student, is to eliminate the need in his life for the college; the task is to help him become a self-educating man.

~ C. Wright Mills

A great deal of learning can be packed into an empty head.

~ Karl Kraus

Opinion is ultimately determined by the feelings, and not by the intellect.

~ Herbert Spencer

To ridicule philosophy is really to philosophize.

~ Blaise Pascal

We receive three educations, one from our parents, one from our schoolmasters, and one from the world. The third contradicts all that the first two teach us.

~ Baron de Montesquieu

Experience is a good teacher, but she sends in terrific bills.

~ Minna Antrim

Most of one's life...is one prolonged effort to prevent oneself thinking.

~ Aldous Huxley

SELF-CONFIDENCE & SELF-WORTH

Happiness depends upon ourselves.

~ Aristotle

The closing years of life are like the end of a masquerade party, when the masks are dropped.

~ Arthur Schopenhauer

To show resentment at a reproach is to acknowledge that one may have deserved it.

~ Cornelius Tacitus

Trust your thinking and have the courage to act on it.

~ Michael E. Kerr

When we ask for advice we are usually looking for an accomplice.

~ Charles Varlet de la Grange

We are always glad when a great man reassures us of his humanity by possessing a few peculiarities.

~ Andre Maurois

Loneliness can be conquered only by those who can bear solitude.

~ Paul Tillich

Parents accept their obsolescence with the best grace they can muster...they do all they can to make it easy for the younger generation to surpass the older, while secretly dreading the rejection that follows.

~ Christopher Lasch

Give me the young man who has brains enough to make a fool of himself.

~ Robert Louis Stevenson

People who do not understand themselves have a craving for understanding.

~ Wilhelm Stekel

If you wish to understand others, you must intensify your own individualism.

~ Oscar Wilde

I think it is not well for any of us to allow another personality to submerge in any way our own.

~ Olive Schreiner

Zeal without knowledge is fire without light.

~ Thomas Fuller

I was thinking of my patients, and how the worst moment for them was when they discovered they were masters of their own fate. It was not a matter of bad or good luck. When they could no longer blame fate, they were in despair.

~ Anais Nin

De Gaulle did not use "writers"; the very idea is grotesque. The leader who allows others to speak for him is abdicating.

~ May Sarton

Even the smallest person can change the course of the future.

~ J.R.R. Tolkien

Advice is what we ask for when we already know the answer but wish we didn't.

~ Erica Jong

Each individual thinks himself the center of the world. Nothing seems more important to us than our own existence.

~ Alexis Carrel

Loneliness and the feeling of being unwanted are the most terrible poverty.

~ Mother Teresa

Men love because they are afraid of themselves, afraid of the loneliness that lives in them, and need someone in whom they can lose themselves as smoke loses itself in the sky.

~ V. F. Calverton

Men are made stronger on realization that the helping hand they need is at the end of their own right arm.

~ Sidney J. Phillips

The greatest happiness is to be that which one is.

~ Theodore Herzl

Many of our fears are tissue-paper-thin, and a single courageous step would carry us through them.

~ Brendan Francis

A diamond with a flaw is better than a common stone that is perfect.

~ Chinese proverb

I don't know the key to success, but the key to failure is trying to please everybody.

~ Bill Cosby

Egotism: the art of seeing in yourself what others cannot see.

~ George Higgins

No man likes to have his intelligence or good faith questioned, especially if he has doubts about himself.

~ Henry Adams

You must not have too much fear of not being up to your task when you are approaching great problems and great works.

~ Georges Duhamel

Man's highest merit always is, as much as possible, to rule external circumstances and as little as possible to let himself be ruled by them.

~ Johann Wolfgang von Goethe

Know thyself.

~ Socrates

If you doubt yourself, then indeed you stand on shaky ground.

~ Henrik Ibsen

I have to live for others and not for myself; that's middle-class morality.

~ George Bernard Shaw

Let America realize that self-scrutiny is not treason. Self-examination is not disloyalty.

~ Richard Cardinal Cushing

Jimmy taught me a long time ago that you do the best you can and don't worry about the criticisms. Once you accept the fact that you're not perfect, then you develop some confidence.

~ Rosalynn Carter

Make the best use of what is in your power, and take the rest as it happens.

~ Epictetus

The thing to do, when one feels sure that he has said or done the right thing, and is condemned, is to stand still and keep quiet. If he is right, time will show it.

~ Booker T. Washington

No man can produce great things who is not thoroughly sincere in dealing with himself.

~ James Russell Lowell

I have tried lately to read Shakespeare, and found it so intolerably dull it nauseated me.

~ Charles Darwin

A wise man always throws himself on the side of his assailants. It is more his interests than it is theirs to find his weak point.

~ Ralph Waldo Emerson

From without, no wonderful effect is wrought within ourselves, unless some interior, responding wonder meets it.

~ Herman Melville

Men never think their fortunes too great, nor their wit too little.

~ Thomas Fuller

Every man has to seek in his own way to make his self more noble and to realize his own true worth.

~ Albert Schweitzer

We shall return to proven ways – not because they are old, but because they are true.

~ Barry Goldwater

Each man must look to himself to teach him the meaning of life. It is not something discovered; it is something molded.

~ Antoine de Saint-Exupery

Solitary trees, if they grow at all, grow strong.

~ Winston Churchill

Be thine own palace, or the world's thy jail.

~ John Donne

A show of envy is an insult to oneself.

~ Yevgeny Yevtushenko

Confidence affects every aspect of our lives because it is the looking glass through which we view ourselves. People who have high levels of confidence generally earn more money because they take on more demanding careers; are more physically fit because they enjoy being competitive in the gym or on the athletic field; and have more satisfying sex lives because they often do it with another person.

~ Dennis Miller

What the collective age wants, allows, and approves is the perpetual holiday from the self.

~ Thomas Mann

The truly proud man is satisfied with his own good opinion, and does not seek to make converts to it.

~ William Hazlitt

Be yourself. Who is better qualified?

~ Frank J. Giblin II

No morality can be founded on authority, even if the authority were divine.

~ A. J. Ayer

The dogmas of the quiet past are inadequate to the stormy present. The occasion is piled high with difficulty, and we must rise to the occasion. As our case is new, so we must think anew and act anew. We must disenthrall ourselves.

~ Abraham Lincoln

Great services are not canceled by one act or by one single error.

~ Benjamin Disraeli

Self-confidence is the first requisite to great undertakings.

~ Samuel Johnson

There are no facts, only interpretations.

~ Friedrich Nietzsche

In our civilization, men are afraid that they will not be men enough and women are afraid that they might be considered only women.

~ Theodor Reik

There is a certain noble pride, through which merits shine brighter than through modesty.

~ Jean Paul Richter

You've got to be brave and you've got to be bold. Brave enough to take your chance on your own discrimination – what's right and what's wrong, what's good and what's bad.

~ Robert Frost

Be content with what you are, and wish not change; not dread your last day, not long for it.

~ Martial

What we call love is the desire to awaken and to keep awake in another's body, heart and mind, the responsibility of flattering, in our place the self -- of which we are not very certain.

~ Paul Geraldy

We're all in this together – by ourselves.

~ Lily Tomlin

An ostentatious man will rather relate a blunder or an absurdity he has committed, than be debarred from talking of his own dear person.

~ Joseph Addison

The joy of life is variety; the tenderest love requires to be renewed by intervals of absence.

~ Samuel Johnson

311

Such as we are made of, such we be.

~ William Shakespeare

To dare to live alone is the rarest courage; since there are so many who had rather meet their bitterest enemy in the field, than their own hearts in their closet.

~ Charles Caleb Colton

Never let the future disturb you. You will meet it, if you have to, with the same weapons of reason which today arm you against the present.

~ Marcus Aurelius

It is in vain to hope to please all alike. Let a man stand with his face in what direction he will, he must necessarily turn his back on one half of the world.

~ George Dennison Prentice

After the game, the king and pawn go into the same box.

~ Italian proverb

The man who has no inner life is the slave of his surroundings.

~ Henri Frederic Amiel

On the dating scene, a guy's confidence can be the key to his attractiveness. And real confidence means not being afraid to show your flaws, vulnerabilities, or imperfections. Before I'd even let my dates into my car, I'd flash them a confident smile and say, "Hey baby, I hope you're ready for a long night of painfully narcissistic introspection punctuated by physical unwieldiness building up to a big impotent crescendo, followed by me weeping in a locked bathroom."

~ Dennis Miller

Every man who attacks my belief diminishes in some degree my confidence in it, and therefore makes me uneasy, and I am angry with he who makes me uneasy.

~ Samuel Johnson

The less I seek my source for some definitive, the closer I am to fine.

~ Amy Ray & Emily Saliers

I am a part of all I have met.

~ Alfred, Lord Tennyson

Two roads diverged in a wood and I
Took the road less traveled by,
And that has made all the difference.

~ Robert Frost

Depend on your rabbit's foot if you will, but remember
it didn't work for the rabbit!

~ R. E. Shay

Without the help of selfishness, the human animal
would never have developed. Egoism is the vine by
which man hoisted himself out of the swamp and
escaped from the jungle.

~ Blaise Cendrars

The physician should not ask the patient if she is sick.

Solitude, though it may be silent as light, is, like light, the mightiest of agencies; for solitude is essential to man. All men come into this world alone; all will leave it alone.

~ Thomas De Quincey

In solitude especially do we begin to appreciate the advantage of living with someone who knows how to think.

~ Jean Jacques Rousseau

We all make mistakes and are imperfect. People can fear looking foolish or being shown to have weaknesses. Everything else but our ethical choices, our moral conduct, can easily be overlooked or chalked up to inexperience, ignorance, or just plain being human. If one's values are well-determined and consistently applied, one ought to feel confident.

One must learn to love oneself...with a wholesome and healthy love, so that one can bear to be with oneself and need not roam.

~ Friedrich Nietzsche

They are never alone that are accompanied with noble thoughts.

~ Sir Philip Sidney

Cursed be the social lies that warp us from the truth.

~ Alfred, Lord Tennyson

A man cannot be comfortable without his own approval.

~ Mark Twain

Self-respect will keep a man from being abject when he is in the power of enemies, and will enable him to feel that he may be in the right when the world is against him.

~ Bertrand Russell

Self-trust is the essence of heroism.

~ Ralph Waldo Emerson

He that listens after what people say of him shall never have peace.

~ Thomas Fuller

The fundamental defect of fathers is that they want their children to be a credit to them.

~ Bertrand Russell

Self-reverence, self-knowledge, self-control, these three alone lead to sovereign power.

~ Alfred, Lord Tennyson

Our entire life, with our final moral code and our precious freedom, consists ultimately in accepting ourselves as we are.

~ Jean Anouilh

Self-reliance, the height and perfection of man, is reliance on God.

~ Ralph Waldo Emerson

If a man has a strong faith he can indulge in the luxury of skepticism.

~ Friedrich Nietzsche

When you are content to be simply yourself and don't compare or compete, everybody will respect you

~ Lao-Tzu

Trust yourself, then you will know how to live.

~ Johann Wolfgang von Goethe

It takes supreme self-confidence to hold on to the almost nonverbal feelings that characterize who we are, how we interact with other people. You might find it uncanny that it also takes supreme confidence to let go of beliefs we have about ourselves, our world and our relationships when we are shown one way or another that we are wrong. Either way, our confidence is on the line, and it could seem injurious to give up beliefs, especially while others are looking on – or worse – showing us our inaccuracy. But failing to be confident out there in the world for fear that we will eventually be wrong is no way to live.

All man's troubles come from not knowing how to sit
still in a room.

~ Blaise Pascal

What others think of us would be of little moment did
it not, when known, so deeply tinge what we think of
ourselves.

~ Lucius Annaeus Seneca

If I am not for myself, who will be?

~ Pirke Avot

You can always get someone to love you – even if you
have to do it yourself.

~ Tom Masson

Ordinary riches can be stolen; real riches cannot. In
your soul are infinitely precious things than cannot be
taken from you.

~ Oscar Wilde

Fear not the anger of the wise to raise;
Those best can bear reproof who merit praise.

~ Alexander Pope

Everyday people are straying away from the church and going back to God.

~ Lenny Bruce

To give a reason for anything is to breed a doubt of it.

~ William Hazlitt

To make a child in your own image is a capital crime, for your image is not worth repeating. The child knows this and you know it. Consequently you hate each other.

~ Karl Shapiro

What has been the effect of religious coercion? To make half the world fools and the other half hypocrites.

~ Thomas Jefferson

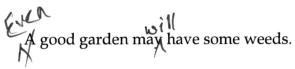
Even A good garden may will have some weeds. ✓

~ Thomas Fuller

It is easy to live for others; everybody does. I call on you to live for yourselves.

~ Ralph Waldo Emerson

Nor is the people's judgment always true:
The most may err as grossly as the few.

~ John Dryden

Be a friend to thyself, and others will be so too.

~ Thomas Fuller

Be wisely selfish.   ✓

~ Dalai Lama

Man is the measure of all things.

~ Protagoras

Independence is for the very few; it is a privilege of the strong.

~ Friedrich Nietzsche

Huge in the human dilemma is not being able to say no.

~ Michael E. Kerr

Here I stand; I can do no other. So help me God.

~ Martin Luther

Until the day of his death, no man can be sure of his courage.

~ Jean Anouilh

Don't know that I will, but until I can find me,
The girl who'll stay and won't play games behind me,
I'll be what I am,
A solitary man.

~ Neil Diamond

It is not what a lawyer tells me I may do; but what humanity, reason, and justice tell me I ought to do.

~ Edmund Burke

It is easy in the world to live after the world's opinion; it is easy in solitude to live after our own; but the great man is he who in the midst of the crowd keep with perfect sweetness the independence of solitude.

~ Ralph Waldo Emerson

Not only do self-love and love of others go hand-in-hand, they are indistinguishable.

~ M. Scott Peck

Self-reverence, self-knowledge, self-control – these three alone lead to sovereign power.

~ Alfred, Lord Tennyson

It is a painful thing
To look at your own trouble and know
That you yourself, and no one else, have made it.

~ Sophocles

Success, recognition, and conformity are the bywords of the modern world, where everyone seems to crave the anesthetizing security of being identified with the majority.

~ Martin Luther King, Jr.

I am not fond of aphorisms... they are one-size-fits-all; each has its opposite, and whatever line of conduct you follow, there is always one to back you up.

~ Alfred de Musset

to be yourself – in a world which is doing its best, night and day, to make you everybody else – means to fight the hardest battle which any human being can fight, and never stop.

~ e. e. cummings

Growing up it all seems so one-sided
Opinions all provided
The future pre-decided
Detached and subdivided
In the mass production zone
Nowhere is the dreamer or the misfit so alone.

~ Neil Peart

Man cannot overestimate the greatness and power of his mind.

~ George Frederick Hegel

I do not feel obliged to believe that the same God who has endowed us with sense, reason, and intellect has intended us to forgo their use.

~ Galileo Galilei

My life is a map; proud ink on olde leather.
Relief depicts the saga of my life:
Love is represented by the mountain.
The river symbolizes pain.
Time is shown by vast grasslands.
The words and symbols make sense to none other than me.

Whenever people agree with me I always feel I must be wrong.

~ Oscar Wilde

Learn what you are, and be such.

~ Pindar

What I must do is all that concerns me, not what the people think.

~ Ralph Waldo Emerson

A fellow who is always declaring he's no fool usually has his suspicions.

~ Wilson Mizner

Allowing yourself to be dependent on another person is the worst possible thing you can do for yourself. You would be better of being dependent on heroin. As long as it's there, it will never let you down. It will always make you happy. But if you expect another person to make you happy, you'll be endlessly disappointed.

~ M. Scott Peck

Why was I born with such contemporaries?

~ Oscar Wilde

Every new adjustment is a crisis in self- esteem.

~ Eric Hoffer

He played the king as if afraid someone else would play the ace.

~ John Mason Brown

Great spirits have always encountered violent opposition from mediocre minds.

~ Albert Einstein

Great spirits encounter opposition from mediocre minds.
Alas, it is difficult to be intellectual among average men.
The unique human may feel alone in a room full of people.
Bittersweet as it may be for honest man, it may never end.

(1st line adapted from A. Einstein)

It is only when one has taken the leap into the unknown of total selfhood, psychological independence, and unique individuality that one is free to proceed along still higher paths of spiritual growth and free to manifest love in its greatest dimensions.

~ M. Scott Peck

My one regret in life is that I am not someone else.

~ Woody Allen

In a mad world only the mad are sane.

~ Akira Kurosawa

Love between persons means that each wants the other to be more himself.

~ M. D'Arcy

Self-respecting people do not care to peep at their reflections in unexpected mirrors, or to see themselves as others see them.

~ Logan Pearsall Smith

It's so hard to find... people who crave intellectualism but also know how to have a good time. My fantasy man has always been a poet on a motorcycle.

~ Lucinda Williams

All charming people have something to conceal, usually their total dependence on the appreciation of others.

~ Cyril Connolly

Einstein's Theories of Relativity were condemned by 100 Nazi professors. His response: "If I were wrong, one professor would have been enough."

I have tried to function as a trusting person and I've been nailed. Now it's me that I don't trust.

~ Carrie Fisher

Would that I could have the integrity
To not feel so lonely about my aloneness…
Rather, to accept it, embrace it.
Because for whatever reason, it is me.

Most people are other people. Their thoughts are someone else's opinions, their lives a mimicry, their passions a quotation.

~ Oscar Wilde

May God defend me from my friends; I can defend myself from my enemies.

~ Voltaire

Do I contradict myself?
Very well, then, I contradict myself,
I am large, I contain multitudes.

~ Walt Whitman

The only thing worse than a man you can't control is a man you can.

~ Margo Kaufman

I won't take my religion from any man who never works except with his mouth.

~ Carl Sandburg

Whenever you find that you are on the side of the majority, it is time to reform.

~ Mark Twain

I have discovered that all human evil comes from this - man's being unable to sit still in a room.

~ Blaise Pascal

An atheist is a man who has no invisible means of support.

~ John Buchan

We are so vain that we even care for the opinion of those we don't care for.

~ Marie Ebner von Eschenbach

Self-love resembles the instrument by which we perpetuate the species. It is necessary, it is dear to us, it gives us pleasure, and it has to be concealed.

~ David Hume

A man of genius has seldom been ruined but by himself.

~ Samuel Johnson

I hate quotations. Tell me what *you* know.

~ Ralph Waldo Emerson

I often quote myself. It adds spice to my conversation.

~ George Bernard Shaw

Awe for nature seems well-placed on God's shoulders, but the next time I kick someone's ass in tennis, teach an exhilarating lesson to children, gaze into the eyes of one of the group home children, achieve an A in a course, land a job, or have an interpersonal connection, perhaps I should exist there, albeit "selfishly," and exalt myself as an individual, as a human. I often attribute the causes of joy to a theistic source, whereas I attribute the darker emotions to my own self.

It is a common delusion that you make things better by talking about them.

~ Dame Rose Macaulay

Computers can figure out all kinds of problems, except the things in the world that just don't add up.

~ James Magary

Be careful where you aim; where you aim you just might hit.

~ Bono

We forfeit three-fourths of ourselves to be like other people.

~ Arthur Schopenhauer

It's curious that I feel so alone on a planet with 5 billion other people.

Half the harm that is done in this world is due to people who want to feel important.

~ T. S. Elliot

Whoso would be a man must be a nonconformist.

~ Ralph Waldo Emerson

To do just the opposite is a form of imitation.

~ Georg Christoph Lichtenberg

Pay no attention to what the critics say; there has never been set up a statue in honor of a critic.

~ Jean Sibelius

Honest criticism is hard to take, particularly from a relative, a friend, an acquaintance, or a stranger.

~ Franklin P. Jones

God will not ask my why I was not Moses, he will ask me why I was not Susya.

~ Rabbi Susya

We are generally the better persuaded by the reasons we discover ourselves than by those given to us by others.

~ Blaise Pascal

Conscience is the inner voice that warns us that someone might be looking.

~ H. L. Mencken

I'm not sure I want popular opinion on my side ~ I've noticed those with the most opinions often have the fewest facts.

~ Bethania McKenstry

I'm no Beethoven, but then again, Beethoven was no me.

When people do not respect us we are sharply offended; yet deep down in his heart no man much respects himself.

~ Mark Twain

TRUTH, JUSTICE &
DEDICATION TO REALITY

Truth is the cry of all, but the game of a few.

~ George Berkeley

Set up as an ideal the facing of reality as honestly and as cheerfully as possible.

~ Karl Menninger

Nothing is easier than self-deceit. For what each man wishes, that he also believes to be true.

~ Demosthenes

Truth is a torch that gleams through the fog without dispelling it.

~ Claude Helvetius

Fate determines many things, no matter how we struggle.

~ Otto Weininger

The truth brings with it a great measure of absolution, always.

~ R. D. Laing

Like all valuable commodities, truth is often counterfeited.

~ James Cardinal Gibbons

What upsets me is not that you lied to me, but that from now on I can no longer believe you.

~ Friedrich Nietzsche

It is a great mistake to fancy oneself greater than one is, and to value oneself at less than one is worth.

~ Johann Wolfgang von Goethe

In the Halls of Justice the only justice is in the halls.

~ Lenny Bruce

Trust only movement. Life happens at the level of events, not or words. Trust movement.

~ Alfred Adler

Life's cruelty strongly indicates the existence of a dispassionate randomness behind the day-to-day happenings of the universe.

There is a way to beat roulette: grab the chips and run.

~ Albert Einstein

There is no instrument so deceptive as the mind.

~ St. John Ervine

To judge wisely, we must know how things appear to the unwise.

~ George Eliot

A superstition is a premature explanation that overstays its time.

~ George Iles

When responsibility is pressed heavily on anyone to make a judgment, it seems to me useful to have as close an understanding of the view of each side as possible.

~ John F. Kennedy

The ultimate test for us of what a truth means is the conduct it dictates or inspires.

~ William James

In a world flagrant with the failures of civilization, what is there particularly immortal about our own?

~ G. K. Chesterton

When a man thinks he is reading the character of another, he is often unconsciously betraying his own.

~ Joseph Farrell

Faith which does not doubt is a dead faith.

~ Miguel de Unamuno

There is something pagan in me that I cannot shake off. In short, I deny nothing, but doubt everything.

~ Lord Byron

In proportion as we perceive and embrace the truth do we become just, heroic, magnanimous, divine.

~ William Lloyd Garrison

Let us, then, be what we are, and speak what we think, and in all things keep ourselves loyal to truth and the sacred professions of friendship.

~ Henry Wadsworth Longfellow

Whatever games are played with us, we must play no games with ourselves, but deal in our privacy with the last honesty and truth. I look upon the simple and child-like virtues of veracity and honesty as the root of all that is sublime in character.

~ Ralph Waldo Emerson

Almost every wise saying has an opposite one, no less wise, to balance it.

~ George Santyana

The well of true wit is truth itself.

~ George Meredith

Injustice is relatively easy to bear; it is justice that hurts.

~ H. L. Mencken

I know myself too well to believe in pure virtue.

~ Albert Camus

Peace if possible, but truth at any rate.

~ Martin Luther

Between whom there is hearty truth, there is love.

~ Henry David Thoreau

Every truth passes through three stages before it is recognized. In the first, it is ridiculed, in the second it is opposed, in the third it is regarded as self-evident.

~ Arthur Schopenhauer

Some people handle the truth carelessly; others never touch it at all.

~ Anonymous

Rough work, iconoclasm, but the only way to get at the truth.

~ Oliver Wendell Holmes

I never did give anybody hell. I just told the truth, and they thought it was hell.

~ Harry S. Truman

Science has proof without any certainty. Creationists have certainty without any proof.

~ Ashley Montague

If anything is poisoning our lives and weakening our society, it is reality – and not the fabrication of television writers and producers.

~ Martin Maloney

Facts do not cease to exist because they are ignored.

~ Aldous Huxley

Pride, perceiving humility honorable, often borrows her cloak.

~ Thomas Fuller

You cannot go against nature,
'Cause when you do,
Go against nature,
It's a part of nature too.

~ Daniel Ash

I tore myself away from the safe comfort of certainties through my love for truth; and truth rewarded me.

~ Simone de Beauvoir

Formerly, when religion was strong and science weak, men mistook magic for medicine; now, when science is strong and religion weak, men mistake medicine for magic.

~ Thomas Szasz

Not believing in force is the same as not believing in gravitation.

~ Leon Trotsky

Poor men's reasons are not heard.

~ Thomas Fuller

You cannot receive a shock unless you have an electric affinity for that which shocks you.

~ Henry David Thoreau

A truth that's told with bad intent beats all the lies you can invent.

~ William Blake

Laws go where dollars please.

~ Portuguese proverb

A clever man commits no minor blunders.

~ Johann Wolfgang von Goethe

Abortion is advocated only by persons who have themselves been born.

~ Ronald Reagan

We always deceive ourselves twice about the people we love – first to their advantage, then to their disadvantage.

~ Albert Camus

The character of human life, like the character of the human condition, like the character of all life, is "ambiguity:" the inseparable mixture of good and evil, true and false, the creative and destructive forces – both individual and social.

~ Paul Tillich

Intelligence is quickness in seeing things as they are.

~ George Santyana

There is no such thing as justice – in or out of the court.

~ Clarence Darrow

And thus I clothe my naked villainy
With odd old ends stolen forth of Holy Writ,
And seem a saint when most I play the devil.

~ William Shakespeare

Slogans are both exciting and comforting, but some of mankind's most terrible misdeeds have been committed under the spell of certain magic words and phrases.

~ James Bryant Conant

Martyrdom has always been proof of the intensity, never the correctness of a belief.

~ Arthur Schnitzler

How could sincerity be a condition of friendship? A taste for truth at any cost is a passion which spares nothing.

~ Albert Camus

The most savage controversies are those about matters to which there is no good evidence either way.

~ Bertrand Russell

Ever since Socrates, playing the sage among fools has been a dangerous business.

~ Denis Diderot

Truth often suffers more by the heat of its defenders than from the arguments of its opponents.

~ William Penn

Ethical axioms are found and tested not very differently from the axioms of science. Truth is what stands the test of experience.

~ Albert Einstein

When the fox preaches, look to your geese.

~ German proverb

Moderation in the pursuit of justice is no virtue.

~ Barry Goldwater

All great truths begin as blasphemies.

~ George Bernard Shaw

When war is declared, truth is the first casualty.

~ Arthur Ponsoby

Respect for the truth is an acquired taste.

~ Mark Van Doren

Time, whose tooth gnaws away everything else, is powerless against truth.

~ T. H. Huxley

Truth is more of a stranger than fiction.

~ Mark Twain

Friendship is almost always the union of a part of one mind with a part of another; people are friends in spots.

~ George Santayana

I have seen no more evident monstrosity and miracle in the world than myself.

~ Michel de Montaigne

We are now in an epoch of wars of religion, but a religion is now called an "ideology."

~ Bertrand Russell

I have seen the science I worshipped and the aircraft I loved destroying the civilization I expected them to serve.

~ Charles A. Lindbergh

Saints should always be judged guilty until they are proven innocent.

~ George Orwell

I can promise to be frank, I cannot promise to be impartial.

~ Johann Wolfgang von Goethe

That which has always been accepted by everyone, everywhere, is almost certain to be false.

~ Paul Valery

Laws are like spiders' webs which, if anything small falls into them they ensnare it, but large things break through and escape.

~ Solon

I maintain that superstition is more hurtful to God than atheism is.

~ Denis Diderot

Time, which strengthens friendship, weakens love.

~ La Bruyere

Things are entirely what they appear to be and *behind them*...there is nothing.

~ Jean Paul Sartre

People don't like the true and simple; they like fairy tales and humbug.

~ Edmond and Jules de Goncourt

Habit with him was all the test of truth,
"It must be right; I've done it from my youth."

~ George Crabbe

Skepticism is the first step toward truth.

~ Denis Diderot

One can only see one side of a coin from any given perspective. The knowledge that there is another side to that coin is a potent bit of knowledge indeed.

Suicide is the sincerest form of criticism life gets.

~ Wilfred Sheed

How dreadful it is when the judge judges wrong.

~ Sophocles

Even the most equitable of men is not permitted to be a judge in his own cause.

~ Blaise Pascal

Doubt is not a pleasant state of mind, but certainty is absurd.

~ Voltaire

I tremble for my country when I reflect that God is just.

~ Thomas Jefferson

The arm of the moral universe is long, but it bends toward justice.

~ Martin Luther King, Jr.

Man does best when controlling urges to aggress and dominate:
An eye for an eye for an eye leaves the whole world blind....
With the incredible advances we have made this century,
Masculinity may explain why a utopian planet earth hard to find-

(the second line by Gandhi)

When you choose the lesser of two evils, always remember that it is still an evil.

~ Max Lerner

The assassinations of the Kennedys and Martin Luther King, Jr. showed that all of the wishing and hoping and holding hands and humming and signing petitions and licking envelopes is a bit futile.

~ George Carlin

With money in your pocket, you are wise, and you are handsome, and you sing well too.

~ Jewish proverb

In reality, hope is the worst of all evils, because it prolongs man's torments.

~ Friedrich Nietzsche

Los Angeles looks more like the City of Demons it seems.
As one of the richest nations we can't even feed our poor.
The silence where forests dwelled is pierced by screams.
Yet we ignore the harsh pounding of danger on our doors.

Mental health is an ongoing dedication to reality at all costs.

~ M. Scott Peck

A lie told often enough becomes the truth.

~ Vladimir Lenin

There are truths that are not for all men, nor for all times.

~ Voltaire

I don't make jokes. I just watch the government and report the facts.

~ Will Rogers

The truth that makes men free is for the most part the truth which men prefer not to hear

~ Herbert Agar

How could St. Thomas Aquinas or Pope Merciless IX know more about God than the boy next door?

What probably distorts everything in life is that one is convinced that one is speaking the truth because one says what one thinks.

~ Sacha Guitry

Misconceptions about love can lead to suffering. For instance, misconceptions like: "falling in love."

~ M. Scott Peck

Convictions are more dangerous foes of truth than lies.

~ Friedrich Nietzsche

Democracy consists of choosing your dictators, after they've told you what you think it is you want to hear.

~ Alan Corenk

If our creator is good, powerful, knowledgeable, and everywhere,
Then how can all manner of evil deeds escape his watchful eye?
As humans torture, deceive, litigate, and abandon their humanity,
What can explain why people suffer silently and then just die?

Appearances are not held to be a clue to the truth. But we seem to have no other.

~ Ivy Compton-Burnett

Famous remarks are very seldom quoted correctly.

~ Simeon Strunsky

I've wrestled with reality for 35 years, and I'm happy, Doctor, I finally won out over it.

~ Jimmy Stewart

Every nation ridicules other nations, and all are right.

~ Arthur Schopenhauer

To die for an idea; it is unquestionably noble. But how much nobler it would be if men died for ideas that were true!

~ H. L. Mencken

Military justice is to justice what military music is to music.

~ Groucho Marx

My atheism, like that of Spinoza, is true piety towards the universe and denies only gods fashioned by men in their own image, to be servants of their human interests.

~ George Santayana

Men occasionally stumble over the truth, but most of them pick themselves up and hurry off as if nothing ever happened.

~ Winston Churchill

A truth that's told with bad intent beats all the lies you can invent.

~ William Blake

I believe that professional wrestling is clean and everything else in the world is fixed.

~ Frank Deford

I hear much of people's calling to punish the guilty, but very few are concerned to clear the innocent.

~ Daniel Defoe

The fact that a believer is happier than a skeptic is no more to the point than the fact than a drunken man is happier than a sober one.

~ George Bernard Shaw

It is one of the maladies of our age to profess a frenzied allegiance to truth in unimportant matters, to refuse consistently to face her where graver issues are at stake.

~ Norman Douglas

Truth exists, only lies have to be invented.

~ George Braque

Contradiction is not a sign of falsity, nor the lack of contradiction a sign of truth.

~ Blaise Pascal

I have no objection to churches so long as they do not interfere with God's work

~ Brooks Atkinson

Justice is the very last thing of all wherewith the universe concerns itself. It is equilibrium that absorbs its attention.

~ Maurice Maeterlinck

A nation is a society united by delusions about its ancestry and by common hatred of its neighbors.

~ W. R. Inge

If you speak the truth, have one foot in the stirrup.

~ Turkish proverb

Maybe this world is another planet's hell.

~ Aldous Huxley

The hopes for peace and justice in this world
Have stretched like the womb of a mother past due.
The symbols of Rome and Christ on a banner unfurled,
Warped into the demonic symbol the vile Nazis flew.

The history of human opinion is scarcely anything more than the history of human errors.

~ Voltaire

Who lies for you will lie against you.

~ Bosnian proverb

Faith is believing what you know ain't so.

~ Mark Twain

A myth is a religion in which no one any longer believes.

~ James Feibleman

The hypocrites are slandering the sacred halls of Truth!

~ Neil Peart

In quarreling, the truth is always lost.

~ Publilius Syrus

Truth is more powerful than God

~ Friedrich Nietzsche

Say not, 'I have found the truth,' but rather, 'I have found a truth.'

~ Kahlil Gibran

Ignorance is preferable to error, and he is less remote from the truth who believes nothing than he who believes what is wrong.

~ Thomas Jefferson

I believe that love of truth is the basis of all real virtue....

~ Bertrand Russell

You're going to have both problems and joy alone and both problems and joy with another person, so which one do you want?

Our repentance is not so much regret for the evil we have done as fear of what may happen to us because of it.

~ Francois, Duc de La Rochefoucauld

The biggest impediment to making judgments about the content of the Bible is that we were not present for one second during the time in which the events were reputed to have taken place. Are the facts being correctly communicated through time and men?

There are times when lying is the most sacred of duties.

~ Eugene Marin Labiche

There is no man so good, who, were he to submit all his thoughts and actions to the law, would not deserve hanging ten times in his life

~ Michel de Montaigne

Everything Hitler did in Nazi Germany was legal.

~ Martin Luther King, Jr.

Judge a man by his questions rather than by his answers.

~ Voltaire

Regarding judgment day: if God is indeed just, I fear not.
There is always the fabled story, held tightly by innocent girls with sweet eyes...
But a wise person must ultimately query
Whether they have been embracing lies.

PASSION, WILLINGNESS TO RISK & OPENNESS TO EMOTION

Love makes of the wisest man a fool, and of the most foolish woman, a sage.

~ Moritz G. Saphir

Death twitches my ear. "Live," he says, "I am coming."

~ Virgil

In order to be utterly happy, the only thing necessary is to refrain from comparing this moment with other moments in the past - which I often did not fully enjoy because I was comparing them with other moments of the future.

~ Andre Gide

Falling in love is good! Just be careful not to fall so hard that you're knocked unconscious.

Artificial manners vanish the moment the natural passions are touched.

~ Maria Edgeworth

Get pleasure out of life... as much as you can. No one ever died from pleasure.

~ Sol Hurok

There is something about the present which we would not exchange, though we were offered a choice of all past ages to live in.

~ Virginia Woolf

If you let yourself be absorbed completely, if you surrender completely to the moments as they pass, you live more richly those moments.

~ Anne Morrow Lindbergh

The greatest waste of money is to keep it.

~ Jackie Gleason

Success is not the result of spontaneous combustion; you must set yourself on fire.

~ Reggie Leach

Ours in an excessively conscious age. We *know* so much, we feel so little.

~ D. H. Lawrence

I recognize that I live now and only now, and I will do what I want to do *this* moment and not what I decided was best for me yesterday.

~ Hugh Prather

My candle burns at both ends;
It will not last the night;
But ah, my foes, and oh, my friends-
It gives a lovely light.

~ Edna St. Vincent Millay

No one, looking back, ever really regrets one of his young enthusiasms. It is the enthusiasms we did not have that we regret.

~ J. W. Mackail

To live is like to love -- all reason is against it, and all healthy instinct for it.

~ Samuel Butler

It is strange what a contempt men have for the joys that are offered them freely.

~ Georges Duhamel

May the devil chase you every day of your life and never catch you.

~ Irish toast

Inspirations never go in for long engagements; they demand immediate marriage to action.

~ Brendan Francis

True, there is some risk, but not acting *is* an action
My old, defunct memories haunt me like tireless ghost
I am writing the same old book again, never transposed
Fresh experiences are perhaps what I need the most.

What matters is not the idea a man holds, but the depth at which he holds it.

~ Ezra Pound

It is only with the heart that one can see rightly; what is essential is invisible to the eye.

~ Antoine de Saint-Exupery

Many a man is afraid of expressing honest emotion because the word "sentimental" frightens him.

~ Hilaire Belloc

They deem me mad because I will not sell my days for gold; and I deem them mad because they think my days have a price.

~ Kahlil Gibran

Those who are quite satisfied sit still and do nothing; those who are not quite satisfied are the sole benefactors of the world.

~ Walter Savage Landor

After 9/11/2001, I have a new outlook and appreciation for life and each new day, as I am more determined to prove that I will not let any one person or group deprive me of my profound love and loyalty to my country and the freedom it provides for all of us.

~ Greg Hahn

To achieve great things we must live as if we were never going to die.

~ Luc de Clapiers de Vauvenargues

How vain it is to sit down and write when you have not stood up to live.

~ Henry David Thoreau

Fortune and Love befriend the bold.

~ Ovid

When thought becomes excessively painful, action is the finest remedy.

~ Salman Rushdie

Every day look at a beautiful picture, read a beautiful poem, listen to some beautiful music, and if possible, say some reasonable thing.

~ Johann Wolfgang von Goethe

Some people never have anything except ideals.

~ E. W. Howe

Inability to love is the central problem, because that inability masks a certain terror – terror of being touched. And if you can't be touched, you can't be changed. And if you can't be changed, you can't be alive.

~ James Baldwin

The greatest intellectual capacities are only found in connection with a vehement and passionate will.

~ Arthur Schopenhauer

Slang is language which takes off its coat, spits on its hands – and goes to work.

~ Carl Sandburg

The difference between our decadence and the Russians' is that while theirs is brutal, our is apathetic.

~ James Thurber

I prefer the errors of enthusiasm to the indifference of wisdom.

~ Anatole France

Little do men perceive what solitude is, and how far it extendeth. For a crowd is not company, and faces are but a gallery of pictures, and talk but a tinkling cymbal, where there is no love.

~ Francis Bacon

Behold the turtle. He only makes progress when he sticks his neck out.

~ James Bryant Conant

I don't really feel my poems are mine at all. I didn't create them out of nothing. I owe them to my relations with other people.

~ Robert Graves

Passions are vices or virtues in their highest powers.

~ Johann W. von Goethe

Technology - the knack of so arranging the world that we do not have to experience it.

~ Max Frisch

When you only have two pennies left in the world, buy a loaf of bread with one, and a lily with the other.

~ Chinese proverb

They who have experienced the ethereal emotion known by man as "love" - akin to lounging on a hammock as a fragrant breeze wafts by in that sunny place in one's soul - know that the absence of it is hardly worth living for.

Happiness makes up in height what it lacks in length.

~ Robert Frost

All our reasoning ends in surrender to feeling.

~ Blaise Pascal

The man who is master of his passions is Reason's slave.

~ Cyril Connolly

Life is action and passion; therefore, it is required of a man that he should share the passion and action of the time, at peril of being judged not to have lived.

~ Oliver Wendell Holmes, Jr.

The tragedy of life is not so much what men suffer, but rather what they miss.

~ Thomas Carlyle

An intense feeling carries with it its own universe, magnificent or wretched as the case may be.

~ Albert Camus

Poetry is a way of taking life by the throat.

~ Robert Frost

What our age lacks is not reflection but passion.

~ Soren Kierkegaard

It is with passions as it is with fire and water – they are good servants but bad masters.

~ Roger l'Estrange

One hour of life, crowded to the full with glorious action, and filled with noble risks, is worth whole years of those mean observances of paltry decorum.

~ Walter Scott

A single event can awaken within us a stranger totally unknown to us. To live is to slowly be born.

~ Antoine de Saint-Exupery

Music is the shorthand of emotion.

~ Leo Tolstoy

A sentimentalist is simply one who desires to have the luxury of an emotion without paying for it.

~ Oscar Wilde

Our judgments about things vary according to the time left us to live – that we think is left us to live.

~ Andre Gide

The mark of a mature man is the ability to give love and receive it joyously and without guilt.

~ Leo Baeck

My advice to those who are about to begin, in earnest, the journey of life, is to take their heart in one hand and a club in the other.

~ Josh Billings

They sicken of the calm who know the storm.

~ Dorothy Parker

Life is ours to be spent, not to be saved.

~ D. H. Lawrence

The Indian Summer of life should be a little sunny and a little sad, like the season, and infinite in wealth and depth of tone – but never hustled.

~ Henry Adams

Don't do things to not die, do things to enjoy living. The by-product may be not dying.

~ Bernard S. Siegel

We should take care not to make intellect our god; it has, of course, powerful muscles, but no personality.

~ Albert Einstein

We are all here for a spell. Get all the good laughs you can.

~ Will Rogers

The superfluous is very necessary.

~ Voltaire

The test of pleasure is the memory it leaves behind.

~ Jean Paul Richter

"Why not?" is a slogan for an interesting life.

~ Mason Cooley

If comfort with aloneness is good, then comfort with togetherness is great.

The knowledge of the world is only to be acquired in the world, and not in a closet.

~ Lord Chesterfield

You are the sun,
I am the moon.
You are the words,
I am the tune.
Play me.

~ Neil Diamond

Beauty is unbearable, drives us to despair, offering us for a minute the glimpse of an eternity that we should like to stretch out over the whole of time.

~ Albert Camus

We should not pretend to understand the world only by the intellect; we apprehend it just as much by feeling. Therefore the judgment of the intellect is, at best, only half of truth, and must, if it be honest, also come to an understanding of its inadequacy.

~ Carl Jung

There is no greater nor keener pleasure than that of bodily love- and none which is more irrational.

~ Plato

The loving are the daring.

~ Bayard Taylor

A good indignation brings out all one's powers.

~ Ralph Waldo Emerson

In Heaven, all the interesting people are missing.

~ Friedrich Nietzsche

Why spend your time worrying about the meaning of life and such when there are so many more important things for us to think about?

Wisdom lies not in reason, but in love.

~ Andre Gide

It is difficult to overcome one's passions, and impossible to satisfy them.

~ Marguerite de La Sabliere

A wholly psychological and almost incurable disease...attacks young, ardent, naïve souls in love with the true and the beautiful,...who discover the evil and ugliness of society.... The disease is suicide.

~ Alfred de Vigny

There is one kind of robber whom the law does not strike at, and who steals what is most precious to men: time.

~ Napoleon Bonaparte

Slums may be breeding-grounds of crime, but middle-class suburbs are incubators of apathy and delirium.

~ Cyril Connolly

Fortune favors the bold.

~ Terence

We may affirm absolutely that nothing great in the world has been accomplished without passion.

~ Georg Wilhelm Friedrich Hegel

Sometimes I think and other times I am.

~ Paul Valery

Money talks. But it don't sing and dance and it don't walk.

~ Neil Diamond

Happy the man, and happy he alone,
He who can call today his own;
He who, secure within, can say,
Tomorrow, do thy worst, for I have lived today.

~ John Dryden

If we open a quarrel between the present and the past, we shall find that we have lost the future.

~ Winston Churchill

O for a life of Sensations rather than of Thoughts!

~ John Keats

Solemnity is the shield of idiots.

~ Baron de Montesquieu

Man is only truly great when he acts from the passions.

~ Benjamin Disraeli

To be able to say how much you love is to love but little.

~ Petrarch

Solitude, the safeguard of mediocrity....

~ Ralph Waldo Emerson

Perhaps passion does not negate objectivity, it emboldens it.

To live alone one must be an animal or god.

~ Friedrich Nietzsche

God make me chaste ... but not yet.

~ St. Augustine

We are never so defenseless against suffering as when we love....

~ Sigmund Freud

Only passions, great passions, can elevate the soul to great things.

~ Denis Diderot

Who reflects too much will accomplish little.

~ Johann von Schiller

People living deeply have no fear of death.

~ Anais Nin

Seize the day!

~ Horace

The supreme happiness in life is the conviction that we are loved.

~ Victor Hugo

Life is either a daring adventure or nothing.... Security is mostly a superstition. It does not exist in nature.

~ Helen Keller

At one point Hitler wanted to be an artist, but, having failed, went on to become the most infamous violator of human rights in history.

To read a writer is for me not merely to get an idea of what he says, but to go off with him and travel in his company.

~ Andre Gide

What some call health, if purchased by perpetual anxiety about diet, isn't much better than tedious disease.

~ George Dennison Prentice

Nothing has a stronger influence psychologically on their environment, and especially on their children, that the unlived lives of the parents.

~ Carl Jung

I compare thee to the moon and stars.
I desire you like only a poet can.
We're a flame that will eternally burn,
With trust and passion as the fan.

There is only one duty: that is to be happy.

~ Denis Diderot

I know of only one duty, and that is to love.

~ Albert Camus

To die is poignantly bitter, but the idea of having to die without having lived is unbearable.

~ Erich Fromm

I call bourgeois anyone who, in a fight or love affair, surrenders for safety's sake. I call bourgeois whoever puts anything ahead of feeling and sentiment.

~ Jean Paul Fargue

I went to the woods because I wished to live deliberately, to front only the essential facts of life, and see if I could not learn what it had to teach, and not, when I came to die, discover that I had not lived.

~ Henry David Thoreau

Disbelief in magic can force a poor soul into believing in government and business.

~ Tom Robbins

Emotion is as admirable as erudition.

My father always used to say that when you die, if you've got five real friends, then you've had a great life.

~ Lee Iacocca

Ask yourself whether you are happy and you cease to be so.

~ John Stuart Mill

Isn't it fitting that blood symbolizes both wounds and familial relationship?

Your friends will know you better in the first minute you meet than your acquaintances will know you in a thousand years.

~ Richard Bach

You are worried about seeing him spend his early years doing nothing. What! It is nothing to be happy?… Never in his life will he be so busy again.

~ Jean Jacques Rousseau

Apart from her, an image lingers in my mind;
A fusion of her, us, and my desires.
Music that mirrors feelings soothe me in her absence;
In the coolness of solitude they are a warm fire.

Summer's going fast, nights growing colder,
Children growing up, old friends growing older,
Freeze this moment a little bit longer,
Make each impression a little bit stronger.

~ Neil Peart

Most people would like to be delivered from
temptation but would like it to keep in touch.

~ Robert Orben

A full life will be full of pain. But the only alternative
is not to live fully, or not to live at all.

~ M. Scott Peck

The heart has its reasons that the reason knows nothing
of.

~ Blaise Pascal

By the time we've made it, we've had it.

~ Malcolm Forbes

Killing time or killing yourself amounts to the same thing, strictly speaking.

~ Elsa Triolet

I fantasize of her as a man imprisoned,
As though her smile hides the key.
Indeed, her intellect frees me from chains,
Her wit allows me to more clearly see.

I have met a lady in the meads
Full beautiful, a faery's child
Her hair was long,
Her foot was light
And her eyes were wild.

~ John Keats

Technology is a way of organizing the universe so that man doesn't have to experience it.

~ Max Frisch

Men who never get carried away should be.

~ Malcolm Forbes

If we choose to be passive, we eat the crumbs from the tables of those who choose to feast on the best this world has to offer. It is only those who use their freedom best who live the life we are here to live to the fullest.

~ Tom Morris

Life is on the wire. Everything else is just waiting.

~ John A. Marshall

Marriage is a wonderful institution. But who wants to live in an institution?

~ Groucho Marx

I believe in getting into hot water; it keeps you clean.

~ G. K. Chesterton

I prefer the errors of enthusiasm to the indifference of wisdom.

~ Anatole France

It's all right letting yourself go as long as you can let yourself back.

~ Mick Jagger

Nobody has ever measured, even poets, how much a heart can hold.

~ Zelda Fitzgerald

Health nuts are going to feel stupid someday, lying in hospitals dying of nothing.

~ Redd Foxx

Live your life such that if you were to die at that very moment you would feel proud to have that described in your epitaph. For example, "So-and-so died while helping an old lady across the street" is considerably preferred over "So-and-so died while engaging in autoerotic asphyxiation."

The young man who has not wept is a savage, and the older man who will not laugh is a fool.

~ George Santayana

Television has proved that people will look at anything rather than each other.

~ Ann Landers

Early to rise and early to bed makes a male healthy and wealthy and dead.

~ James Thurber

Why live in a such a narrow bandwidth,
When the full range can be enjoyed?
Why not choose to seize the day forthwith,
And embrace, rather than avoid?

The person who has lived the most is not the one with the most years, but the one with the richest experiences.

~ Jean Jacques Rousseau

Too much of a good thing is wonderful.

~ Mae West

He who fights with monsters should look to it that he himself does not become a monster. And when you gaze long into an abyss, the abyss also gazes into you.

~ Friedrich Nietzsche

Virtue is bold, and goodness never fearful.

~ William Shakespeare

Why view the world two-dimensionally,
When three glorious dimensions exist?
Why not wonder unconventionally,
Choosing to *live* rather than just persist?

Whatever you can do, or dream you can, begin it.
Boldness has genius, power, and magic in it.

~ Johann Wolfgang von Goethe

When we shy away from death, the ever-changing nature of things, we inevitably shy away from life.

~ M. Scott Peck

Is there life before death?

~ Graffiti, in Belfast

Alas, I live an unexamined life.
Socrates would most certainly look upon me with contempt-
Though I may desire more excitement,
I oft' bow to inertia and fail to make any attempt.
We let sand pass through the hourglass as though it is limitless.

No man is an island, entire of itself; every man is a piece of the continent, a part of the main.

~ John Donne

They do not love that do not show their love.

~ William Shakespeare

Life resembles the banquet of Damocles; the sword is ever suspended.

~ Voltaire

Hold a true friend with both your hands.

~ Nigerian Proverb

In spite of the cost of living, it's still popular.

~ Laurence J. Peter

Life can only be understood backwards; but it must be lived forwards.

~ Soren Kierkegaard

The somewhat shallow life I lead, albeit pleasant,
Seems more like meaningless and dull from one point of view.
Real friendships punctuate it with camaraderie and anxiety;
It turns my pastel existence to a more vibrant hue.

Where I am, death is not; where death is, I am not.
Therefore, death is nothing to me.

~ Lucretius

I went on a diet, swore off drinking and heavy eating,
and in fourteen days I had lost exactly two weeks.

~ Joe E. Lewis

The little emotions are the great captains of our lives
and we obey them without realizing it.

~ Vincent Van Gogh

Consistency is the last refuge of the unimaginative.

~ Oscar Wilde

The tragedy of life is not so much what men suffer, but
what they miss.

~ Thomas Carlyle

At times I am so shocked by the behavior or humanity that I am insulted to have been brought into this world. Other times, I get down on one knee, just thankful I'm alive.

Security is mostly an illusion. It does exist in nature, nor does human kind as a whole experience it. Avoiding danger is no safer in the long run than outright exposure. Life is either a daring adventure or nothing.

~ Helen Keller

HUMOR, LIGHTHEARTEDNESS
&
ACCEPTANCE OF THE ABSURD

When you sit with a nice girl for two hours, you think it's only a minute. But when you sit on a hot stove for a minute, you think it's two hours. That's relativity.

~ Albert Einstein

No mind is thoroughly well organized that is deficient in a sense of humor.

~ Samuel Taylor Coleridge

In America we let people in prison read, study law, even work out, so they can get themselves out of jail in much better mental and physical shape to resume their lives of crime.

~ Dennis Miller

I have too much respect for the idea of God to make it responsible for such an absurd world.

~ Georges Duhamel

It is to be believed because it is absurd.

~ Quintus Septimus Tertullianus

The comic, more than the tragic, because it ignites hope, leads to more, not less, participation in the struggle for a just world.

~ Harvey Cox

A citizen of America will cross the ocean to fight for democracy, but won't cross the street to vote in a national election.

~ Bill Vaughan

Humans are the only animals that have children on purpose, with the exception of guppies, who like to eat theirs.

~ P. J. O'Rourke

In this job, you have only two choices: you are either funny deliberately or you are funny unintentionally.

~ Henry Kissinger

A woman may very well form a friendship with a man, but for this to endure, it must be assisted by a little physical antipathy.

~ Friedrich Nietzsche

We have met the enemy, and he is us.

~ Pogo

We should live and learn; but by the time we've learned, it's too late to live.

~ Carolyn Wells

There is only one thing a philosopher can be relied upon to do, and that is to contradict other philosophers.

~ William James

People say life is the thing, but I prefer reading.

~ Logan Pearsall

We hang the petty thieves and appoint the great ones to public office.

~ Aesop

In the fight between you and the world, back the world.

~ Frank Zappa

God made everything out of nothing, but the nothingness shows through.

~ Paul Valery

The various modes of worship, which prevailed in the Roman world, were considered by the people, as equally true; by the philosopher, as equally false; and by the magistrate, as equally useful.

~ Edward Gibbon

There are only two ways of telling the complete truth – anonymously and posthumously.

~ Thomas Sowell

Nothing endures but change.

~ Heraclitus

Two kinds of people: the just, who consider themselves sinners, and the sinners, who consider themselves just.

~ Blaise Pascal

While there is a chance of the world getting through its troubles, I hold that a reasonable man has to behave as though he were sure of it. If at the end your cheerfulness is not justified, at any rate you will have been cheerful.

~ H. G. Wells

A hospital is a dangerous place to be if you're ill.

~ Bill Puett

On my good days I'm agnostic; on my bad days I'm an atheist.

~ Sholeh Iravantchi

Another reason America's great is because we create things here, things of unique beauty. Things that unconsciously interweave the American attributes of ingenuity, optimism, gluttony and narrow-mindedness. Things like "All You Can Eat" restaurants, the Clapper, street legal semi-automatic grenade weapons, the temporary insanity plea, cutting-edge CD-ROM technology used for porno, deep fried cheese, bans on toy guns, rain ponchos for dogs, Orange Julius, Orange County, beer can hats, plea bargaining, and being able to plug your parents with bullets and getting acquitted.

~ Dennis Miller

Comedy is allied to justice.

~ Aristophanes

A little nonsense now and then, is cherished by the wisest men.

~ Roald Dahl

The most pleasant and useful persons are those who leave some of the problems of the universe for God to worry about.

~ Don Marquis

It is never safe to be nostalgic about something until you're absolutely certain there's no chance of its coming back.

~ Bill Vaughn

Parenthood: That state of being better chaperoned than you were before marriage.

~ Marcelene Cox

The real originals now are the people who behave properly.

~ Edith Sitwell

It frees you from doing things you dislike. Since I dislike doing nearly everything, money is handy.

~ Groucho Marx

The chief reason why marriage is rarely a success is that it is contracted while the partners are insane.

~ Joseph Collins

I do not have a psychiatrist and I do not want one, for the simple reason that if he listened to me long enough, he might become disturbed.

~ James Thurber

You can't make up anything anymore. The world itself is a satire. All you're doing is recording it.

~ Art Buchwald

Women are never stronger than when they arm themselves with their weakness.

~ Marie de Vichy-Chamrond

Everything in the world may be endured except continued prosperity.

~ Johann Wolfgang von Goethe

Criminal: A person with predatory instincts who has not sufficient capital to form a corporation.

~ Howard Scott

The gambling known as business looks with austere disfavor upon the business known as gambling.

~ Ambrose Bierce

People who work sitting down get paid more than people who work standing up.

~ Ogden Nash

The man who reads nothing at all is better educated than the man who reads nothing but newspapers.

~ Thomas Jefferson

It's going to be fun to watch and see how long the meek can keep the earth after they've inherited it.

~ Kin Hubbard

Now and then an innocent man is sent to the legislature.

~ Kin Hubbard

Intelligence is characterized by a natural inability to understand life.

~ Henri Bergson

Economics is extremely useful as a form of employment for economists.

~ John Kenneth Galbraith

Some men are born mediocre, some men achieve mediocrity, and some men have mediocrity thrust upon them.

~ Joseph Heller

Love is like those second-rate hotels where all he luxury is in the lobby.

~ Paul-Jean Toulet

Man is harder than rock and more fragile than an egg.

~ Yugoslavian proverb

Life is easier that you'd think; all that is necessary is to accept the impossible, do without the indispensable, and bear the intolerable.

~ Kathleen Norris

Woman begins by resisting a man's advances and ends by blocking his retreat.

~ Oscar Wilde

I am a kind of paranoiac in reverse. I suspect people of plotting to make me happy.

~ J. D. Salinger

Have you ever noticed? Anybody going slower than you is an idiot, and anyone going faster than you is a moron.

~ George Carlin

It's no longer a question of staying healthy. It's a question of finding a sickness you like.

~ Jackie Mason

A sense of humor is part of the art of leadership, of getting along with people, of getting things done.

~ Dwight D. Eisenhower

If a little knowledge is dangerous, where is the man who has so much as to be out of danger?

~ Thomas Henry Huxley

It takes a lot of things to prove you are smart, but only one thing to prove you are ignorant.

~ Don Herold

A dirty joke is not, of course, a serious attack upon morality, but it is a sort of mental rebellion, a momentary wish that things were otherwise.

~ George Orwell

412

Comedy is simply a funny way of being serious.

~ Peter Ustinov

In order to preserve your self-respect, it is sometimes necessary to lie and cheat.

~ Robert Byrne

Lack of money is the root of all evil.

~ George Bernard Shaw

Ever notice when you blow in a dog's face he gets mad at you, but when you take him in a car he sticks his head out the window?

~ George Carlin

In every dispute between parent and child, both cannot be right, but they may be, and usually are, both wrong. It is this situation which gives family life its peculiar hysterical charm.

~ Isaac Rosenfeld

I remain just one thing and one thing only, and that is a clown. It places me on a far higher plane than any politician.

~ Charlie Chaplin

Men will take almost any kind of criticism except the observation that they have no sense of humor.

~ Steve Allen

If ignorance is bliss, why aren't there more happy people?

~ Anonymous

I admire the serene assurance of those who have religious faith. It is wonderful to observe the calm confidence of a Christian with four aces.

~ Mark Twain

Death is for many of us the gate of hell; but we are inside on the way out, not on the way in.

~ George Bernard Shaw

When you're safe at home, you wish you were having an adventure. When you're having an adventure, you wish you were safe at home.

~ Thornton Wilder

Small children disturb your sleep, big children your life.

~ Yiddish proverb

I have found some of the best reasons I ever had for remaining at the bottom simply by looking at the men at the top.

~ Frank Moore Colby

Hate is a kind of "passive suffering" but indignation is a kind of joy.

~ William Butler Yeats

Conscience is the inner voice that tells us someone may be looking.

~ H. L. Mencken

If congressmen talk too much, how can it be otherwise in a body to which the people send one hundred and fifty lawyers, whose trade it is to question everything, yield nothing, and talk by the hour?

~ Thomas Jefferson

The banalities of a great man pass for wit.

~ Alexander Chase

Every man is a damn fool for at least five minutes every day; wisdom consists in not exceeding the limit.

~ Elbert Hubbard

There are no atheists in the foxholes.

~ William Thomas Cummings

I wish to become rich, so that I can instruct the people and glorify honest poverty, like those kind-hearted, fat, benevolent people do.

~ Mark Twain

If a man has no vices, he's in great danger of making vices of his virtues, and there's a spectacle.

~ Thornton Wilder

More than just silliness or stupidity, a vivid sense of humor can yield insight into a person's modesty, passion, and intelligence.

Stoop and you'll be stepped on; stand tall and you'll be shot at.

~ Carlos A. Urbizo

Why is it that our memory is good enough to retain the least triviality that happens to us, and yet not good enough to recollect how often we have told it to the same person?

~ Francois, Duc de La Rochefoucauld

If the human race wants to go to Hell in a handbasket, technology can help it get there by jet.

~ Charles M. Allen

There was a time when we expected nothing of our children but obedience, as opposed to the present, when we expect everything of them but obedience.

~ Anatole Broyard

Look for the ridiculous in everything, and you will find it.

~ Jules Renard

The intelligent man finds almost everything ridiculous, the sensible man hardly anything.

~ Johann Wolfgang von Goethe

Good judgment comes from experience, and experience comes from bad judgment.

~ Barry LePatner

Society is composed of two great classes: those who have more dinners than appetite, and those who have more appetite than dinners.

~ Sebastien Chamfort

An honest politician is one who, when he is bought, will stay bought.

~ Simon Cameron

Any woman who thinks the way to a man's heart is through his stomach is aiming about 10 inches too high.

~ Adrienne E. Gusoff

Fortune smiles at some, and laughs at others.

~ Gene English

Wit is the sudden marriage of ideas which, before their union, were not perceived to have any relation.

~ Mark Twain

One is healthy when one can laugh at the earnestness and zeal with which one has been hypnotized by any single detail of one's life.

~ Friedrich Nietzsche

Christianity might be a good thing if anyone ever tried it.

~ George Bernard Shaw

I think if you ask people what their concept of heaven is, they would say, if they are honest, that it is a big department store, with new things every week – all the money to buy them, and maybe a little more than their neighbors.

~ Erich Fromm

An indecent mind is a perpetual feast.

~ Old saying

Reformers have the idea that change can be achieved through brute sanity.

~ George Bernard Shaw

Tragedy is when I cut my finger. Comedy is when you walk into an open sewer and die.

~ Mel Brooks

I have found the best way to give advice to your children is to find out what they want and then advise them to do it.

~ Harry S. Truman

The whole object of comedy is to be yourself; and the closer you get to that, the funnier you will be.

~ Jerry Seinfeld

If you talk to God, you are praying; if God talks to you, you have schizophrenia.

~ Thomas Szasz

If absolute power corrupts absolutely, where does that leave God?

~ George Daacon

Once a man would spend a week patiently waiting if he missed a stagecoach, but now he rages if he misses the first section of a revolving door.

~ Simeon Strunsky

The poor don't know that their function in life is to exercise our generosity.

~ Jean-Paul Sartre

Millions long for immortality who do not know what to do with themselves on a rainy Sunday afternoon.

~ Susan Ertz

Gluttony is an emotional escape, a sign something is eating us.

~ Peter de Vries

If you make people think they're thinking, they'll love you; but if you really make them think, they'll hate you.

~ Don Marquis

Democracy means government by discussion, but it is only effective if you can stop people talking.

~ Clement Atlee

What a good thing Adam had - when he said a good thing, he knew nobody had said it before.

~ Mark Twain

The most protean aspect of comedy is its potentiality for transcending itself, for responding to the conditions of tragedy by laughing in the darkness.

~ Harry Levin

The world gets better every day - then worse again in the evening.

~ Kin Hubbard

I am going to give my psychoanalyst one more year, then I'm going to Lourdes.

~ Woody Allen

Life is better than death, I believe, if only because it is less boring and because it has fresh peaches in it.

~ Thomas Walker

There is never enough time, unless you're serving it.

~ Malcolm Forbes

Take everything you like seriously, except yourselves.

~ Rudyard Kipling

Isn't it interesting that the same people who laugh at science fiction listen to weather forecasts and economists?

~ Kelvin Throop III

At any given moment life is completely senseless. But viewed over a period, it seems to reveal itself as an organism existing in time, having a purpose, tending in a certain direction.

~ Aldous Huxley

Life is pleasant. Death is peaceful. It's the transition that's troublesome.

~ Isaac Asimov

The first half of our lives is ruined by our parents and the second half by our children.

~ Clarence Darrow

Comedy is a socially acceptable form of hostility. That is what comics do, stand the world upside down.

~ George Carlin

Watching corporate America these days is like watching drunks at a revival meeting, vowing to sin no more.

~ Allan Sloan

A humorist is a man who feels bad but feels good about it.

~ Don Herold

There are things of deadly earnest that can only be safely mentioned under cover of a joke.

~ J. J. Procter

We are all here on earth to help others; what on earth others are here for I don't know.

~ W. H. Auden

Let us be thankful for the fools. But for them the rest of us could not succeed.

~ Mark Twain

The government is concerned about the population explosion, and the population is concerned about the government explosion.

~ Ruth Rankin

Sure there are dishonest men in local government. But there are dishonest men in national government too.

~ Richard M. Nixon

So far as I can remember, there is not one word in the Gospels in praise of intelligence.

~ Bertrand Russell

The secret of eternal youth is arrested development.

~ Alice R. Longworth

Experience is the name so many people give to their mistakes.

~ Oscar Wilde

If you live long enough, the venerability factor creeps in; you get accused of things you never did and praised for virtues you never had.

~ I. F. Stone

Pointing out the comic elements of a situation can bring a sense of proportion and perspective to what might otherwise seem an overwhelming problem.

~ Harvey Mindess

In our society...those who are in reality superior in intelligence can be accepted by their fellows only if they pretend they are not.

~ Marya Mannes

I make the most of all that comes,
And the least of all that goes.

~ Sarah Teasdale

She had lost the art of conversation, but not, unfortunately, the power of speech.

~ George Bernard Shaw

Vexed sailors cursed the rain
For which poor shepherds prayed in vain.

~ Edmund Waller

Wasting one's youth is better than doing nothing at all with it.

~ Georges Courteline

A satirist is a man who discovers unpleasant things about himself and then says them about other people.

~ Peter McArthur

He who laughs, lasts.

~ Anonymous

To attain the truth, we ought always to believe that what seems white is black if the Hierarchical Church so defines it.

~ Ignatius Loyola

Satire should, like a polished razor keen,
Wound with a touch that's scarcely felt or seen.

~ Mary Wortley Montagu

Many of the insights of the saint stem from his experience as a sinner.

~ Eric Hoffer

Insane people are always sure they're just fine. It's only the sane people who are willing to admit they're crazy.

~ Nora Ephron

Women have a special talent for understanding men better than he understands himself.

~ Victor Hugo

Man is certainly stark mad: he cannot make a flea, yet he makes gods by the dozens.

~ Michel de Montaigne

It is easier to rule a kingdom than to regulate a family.

~ Japanese proverb

Sin is a dangerous toy in the hands of the virtuous. It should be left to the congenitally sinful, who know when to play with it and when to let it alone.

~ H. L. Mencken

The sensibility of man to trifles, and his insensibility to great things, indicates a strange inversion.

~ Blaise Pascal

There can be no high civilization where there is not ample leisure.

~ Henry Ward Beecher

God will provide - if only God would provide until he provides.

~ Hanan J. Ayalti

People who say they sleep like a baby usually don't have one.

~ Leo J. Burke

When man wantonly destroys a work of man we call his a vandal; when a man destroys one of the works of God, we call him a sportsman.

~ Joseph Wood Krutch

I'll not listen to reason.... Reason always means what someone else has to say.

~ Elizabeth Gaskell

You go to a psychiatrist when you're slightly cracked up and keep going until you're completely broke.

~ Anonymous

The excess of a virtue is a vice.

~ Greek proverb

All who are not of good race in this world are chaff.

~ Adolf Hitler

My only policy is to profess evil and do good.

~ George Bernard Shaw

He that jokes confesses.

~ Italian proverb

Nonviolence is a flop. The only bigger flop is violence.

~ Joan Baez

I respect only those who resist me, but I cannot tolerate them.

~ Charles de Gaulle

Women are never disarmed by compliments; men always are.

~ Oscar Wilde

Your theory is crazy, but it's not crazy enough to be true.

~ Niels Bohr

The secret of humor... is not joy but sorrow. There is no humor in heaven.

~ Mark Twain

There is more logic in humor than in anything else. Because, you see, humor is truth.

~ Victor Borge

We owe to the Middle Ages the two worst inventions of humanity - romantic love and gunpowder.

~ Andre Maurois

Not by wrath does one kill but by laughter.

~ Friedrich Nietzsche

Do unto yourself as your neighbors do unto themselves and look pleasant.

~ George Ade

There is no human problem which could not be solved if people would simply do as I advise.

~ Gore Vidal

If the Prince of Peace should come to this earth, one of the first things he would do would be to put psychiatrists in their place.

~ Aldous Huxley

The absurd is born of the confrontation between the human call and the unreasonable silence of the world.

~ Albert Camus

On one issue at least, men and women agree; they both distrust women.

~ H. L. Mencken

If presidents don't do it to their wives, they do it to their country.

~ Mel Brooks

I think everything is very, very heavy so I always joke about everything.

~ Carrie Fisher

We do not have to visit a madhouse to find disordered minds; our planet is the mental institution of the universe.

~ Johann Wolfgang von Goethe

If absolute power corrupts absolutely, does absolute powerlessness make you pure?

~ Harry Shearer

The only way to get a serious message across is through comedy.

~ Woody Harrelson

I never knew a man in my life who could not bear another's misfortunes perfectly like a Christian.

~ Alexander Pope

Everything is funny as long as it is happening to somebody else.

~ Will Rogers

A gentleman never insults anyone unintentionally.

~ Oscar Wilde

You must first have a lot of patience to learn to have patience.

~ Stanislaw J. Lec

For a list of all the ways technology has failed to improve the quality of life, please press three.

~ Alice Kahn

The love of truth lies at the root of much humor.

~ Robertson Davies

Comedy is as profound as philosophy.

A difference in taste in jokes is a great strain on the affections.

~ George Elliot

Children today are tyrants. They contradict their parents, gobble their food, and tyrannize their teachers.

~ Socrates

Laughter is the shortest distance between two people.

~ Victor Borge

The odds against there being a bomb on a plane are a million to one, and against two bombs a million times a million to one. Next time you fly, cut the odds and take a bomb.

~ Benny Hill

In all matters of opinion, our adversaries are insane.

~ Oscar Wilde

What should the reasonable woman make of this world?
If God is omniscient, omnipresent, omnipotent, and benevolent,
Why does his creation – wondrous human beings,
Face atrocity wrought by nature unbridled and humans malevolent?

The only thing that can stop a teenage boy is a teenage girl.

~ Robert Transpota

You can't say civilization isn't advancing: in every war they kill you in a new way.

~ Will Rogers

"White trash" is a term that can be used for ignorant, classless and poor white people, as well as for ignorant, classless and rich white people.

Psychiatry enables us to correct our faults by confessing our parents' shortcomings.

~ Laurence J. Peter

April 1. This is the day upon which we are reminded of what we are on the other three hundred and sixty-four.

~ Mark Twain

I'm astounded by people who want to 'know' the universe when it's hard enough to find your way around Chinatown.

~ Woody Allen

What a fine comedy this world would be if one did not play a part in it.

~ Denis Diderot

Ahhh. A man with a sharp wit. Someone ought to take it away from him before he cuts himself.

~ Peter da Silva

Suburbia is where the developer bulldozes out the trees, then names the streets after them.

~ Bill Vaughan

Anyone who goes to a psychiatrist ought to have his head examined.

~ Samuel Goldwyn

Half our life is spent trying to find something to do with the time we have rushed through life trying to save.

~ Will Rogers

The good professor was rare, yet untrustworthy, like a dog that licked your hand but had a history of biting.

~ Chris Offutt

Fun is as deep as seriousness.

I loathe people who keep dogs. They are cowards who haven't got the guts to bite people themselves.

~ August Strindberg

There must be more to life than having everything.

~ Maurice Sendak

Humor is an affirmation of dignity, a declaration of man's superiority to all that befalls him.

~ Romain Gary

Somebody has to do something, and it's just incredibly pathetic that it has to be us.

~ Jerry Garcia

The great thing about democracy is that it gives every voter a chance to do something stupid.

~ Art Spander

Ninety percent of the politicians give the other ten percent a bad name.

~ Henry Kissinger

Money, to be worth striving for, must have blood and perspiration on it - preferably that of someone else.

~ Wilson Mizner

The big difference between sex for money and sex for free is that sex for money usually costs a lot less.

~ Brendan Behan

I stopped voting when I stopped taking drugs. I believe both of those acts are closely related to delusional behavior.

~ George Carlin

My idea of an agreeable person is a person who agrees with me.

~ Benjamin Disraeli

In America any boy may become President, and I suppose it's just one of the risks he takes.

~ Adlai E. Stevenson Jr.

I've always thought that good true sense requires one to see and comment upon the ridiculous.

~ John Kenneth Galbraith

A liberal is a man too broadminded to take his own side in a quarrel.

~ Robert Frost

If there is anything the nonconformist hates worse than a conformist, it's another nonconformist who doesn't conform to the prevailing standard of nonconformity.

~ Bill Vaughan

Are you not scared by seeing that the gypsies are more attractive to us than the apostles?

~ Ralph Waldo Emerson

What if everything is an illusion and nothing exists? In that case, I definitely overpaid for my carpet.

~ Woody Allen

A politician is a man who will double cross that bridge when he comes to it.

~ Oscar Levant

I don't want any yes-men around me. I want everybody to tell me the truth, even if it costs them their jobs.

~ Sam Goldwyn

I have enough money to last me the rest of my life unless I buy something.

~ Jackie Mason

Money can't make me happy, but I sure would be in a bad mood if I didn't have any.

Comedy is essentially a miracle. I believe I'm as important to society as a doctor; to create laughter creates magic. These days nothing is more important.

~ Kathleen Freeman

Life is far too important a thing ever to talk seriously about.

~ Oscar Wilde

Glory be to God, who determined, for reasons we know not, that wickedness and stupidity should rule the world.

~ Arthur de Gobineau

Humor is the most engaging cowardice. With it myself I have been able to hold some of my enemy in play far out of gunshot.

~ Robert Frost

Life does not cease to be funny when people die any more than it ceases to be serious when people laugh.

~ George Bernard Shaw

Analyzing humor is like dissecting a frog. Few people are interested and the frog dies of it.

~ E. B. White

Thank God men cannot as yet fly and lay waste to the sky as well as the earth!

~ Henry David Thoreau

In all comedy there is something regressive that takes us back to the world of play that we first knew as children.

~ Roger Polhemus

They say that God is everywhere, and yet we always think of Him as somewhat of a recluse.

~ Emily Dickinson

It is the wretchedness of being rich that you have to live with rich people.

~ Logan Pearsall Smith

It is hard enough to remember my opinions, without also remembering my reasons for them!

~ Friedrich Nietzsche

Nonsense is an assertion of man's spiritual freedom in spite of all the oppressions of circumstance.

~ Aldous Huxley

I have learnt silence from the talkative, toleration from the intolerant, and kindness from the unkind; yet strange, I am ungrateful to these teachers.

~ Kahlil Gibran

Alas, I am dying beyond my means.

~ Oscar Wilde (sipping champagne on his deathbed)

The poor man is not free to dine at the Ritz.

~ R. H. Tawney

The most incomprehensible thing about the world is that it is at all comprehensible.

~ Albert Einstein

God created sex. Priests created marriage.

~ Voltaire

One doesn't have a sense of humor. It has you.

~ Larry Gelbart

Laughter is the closest thing to the grace of God.

~ Karl Barth

Sleep, riches, and health to be truly enjoyed must be interrupted.

~ Jean Paul Richter

Not a shred of evidence exists in favor of the idea that life is serious.

~ Brendan Gill

I have never made but one prayer to God, a very short one: 'O Lord, make my enemies ridiculous.' And God granted it.

~ Voltaire

I hate mankind, for I think myself one of the best of them, and I know how bad I am.

~ Samuel Johnson

When you go into court you are putting your fate into the hands of twelve people who weren't smart enough to get out of jury duty.

~ Norm Crosby

Man is the only animal that laughs and has a state legislature.

~ Samuel Butler

The "Jerry Springer Show" is like the canary in the mine of our culture: If the canary isn't dead, it's certainly coughing.

~ Phil Donahue

Get all the fools on your side and you can be elected to anything.

~ Frank Dane

The trouble with born-again Christians is that they are an even bigger pain the second time around.

~ Herb Caen

The last time somebody said, 'I find I can write much better with a word processor', I replied, 'They used to say the same thing about drugs.'

~ Roy Blount, Jr.

God is a comedian playing to an audience too afraid to laugh.

~ Voltaire

Faces we see, hearts we know not.

~ Spanish proverb

Your true value depends entirely on what you are compared with.

~ Bob Wells

Reality is a crutch for people who can't cope with drugs.

~ Lily Tomlin

An intellectual is a man who takes more words than necessary to tell more than he knows.

~ Dwight D. Eisenhower

I used to wake up at 4 A.M. and start sneezing, sometimes for five hours. I tried to find out what sort of allergy I had but finally came to the conclusion that it must be an allergy to consciousness.

~ James Thurber

What can you say about a society that says that God is dead and Elvis is alive?

~ Irv Kupcinet

There's a fine line between genius and insanity. I have erased this line.

~ Oscar Levant

I was thrown out of college for cheating on the metaphysics exam; I looked into the soul of the boy sitting next to me.

~ Woody Allen

This is no time to make new enemies.

~ Voltaire (when asked to forswear Satan, on his deathbed)

I was perplexed to discover that Hitler was an avid enthusiast of jokes. How could the same person who decided who should and shouldn't die really value humor?

The average man, who does not know what to do with his life, wants another one which will last forever.

~ Anatole France

I hate to advocate drugs, alcohol, violence, or insanity to anyone, but they've always worked for me.

~ Hunter S. Thompson

Beggars should be abolished. It annoys one to give to them, and it annoys one not to give to them.

~ Friedrich Nietzsche

Men show their character in nothing more clearly than by what they think laughable.

~ Johann Wolfgang von Goethe

I don't necessarily agree with everything I say.

~ Marshall McLuhan

OTHER TRENCHANT THOUGHTS

The world is a comedy for those who think and a tragedy for those who feel.

~ Horace Walpole

A man of action forced into a state of thought is unhappy until he can get out of it.

~ John Galsworthy

Simple pleasures...are the last refuge of the complex.

~ Oscar Wilde

Love your neighbor, yet pull not down your hedge.

~ George Herbert

To turn $100 into $110 is work. To turn $100 million into $110 million is inevitable.

~ Edgar Bronfman

Speech is conveniently located midway between thought and action, where it often substitutes for both.

~ John Andrew Holmes

What a day may bring, a day may take away.

~ Thomas Fuller

Thinkers prepare the revolution; bandits carry it out.

~ Mariano Azuela

Failure changes for the better, success for the worse.

~ Lucius Annaeus Seneca

One cloud is enough to eclipse all the sun.

~ Thomas Fuller

Two things a man cannot hide: that he his drunk, and that he is in love.

~ Antiphanes

Nobody does nothing for nobody for naught.

~ Peter Lord

The conspicuously wealthy urge the character-building value of privation for the poor.

~ John Kenneth Gallbraith

Where there is love, there is pain.

~ Spanish proverb

He who is slowest in making a promise is most faithful in its performance.

~ Jean Jacques Rousseau

Fortune is fickle and soon asks back what he has given.

~ Latin proverb

The flesh endures the storms of the present alone; the mind, those of the past and future as well as the present.

~ Epicurus

The three great elements of modern civilization: Gunpowder, Printing, and the Protestant Religion.

~ Thomas Carlyle

Some are born to sweet delight,
Some are born to endless night.

~ William Blake

Literature is mostly about having sex and not much about having children; life is the other way around.

~ David Lodge

Alas! The love of women! It is known
To be a lovely and a fearful thing.

~ Lord Byron

How different the new order would b
consult the veteran instead of the politic

~ Henry Miller

There is no greater error of Romanticism than the
supposed usefulness of suffering.

~ Robert Brasillach

The physicists have known sin; and that is a
knowledge they cannot lose.

~ J. Robert Oppenheimer

Most people get a fair amount of fun out of their lives,
but on balance life is suffering, and only the very
young or the very foolish imagine otherwise.

~ George Orwell

There is radicalism in all getting, and conservatism in
all keeping. Lovemaking is radical while marriage is
conservative.

~ Eric Hoffer

:ontend with a man who has nothing to lose.

~ Baltasar Gracian

The successful revolutionary is a statesman, the unsuccessful one a criminal.

~ Erich Fromm

Republicans are the party that says government doesn't work, and then they get elected and prove it.

~ P. J. O'Rourke

...it is still possible to look back with some admiration on the Protestant elite, despite the racism, anti-Semitism, and rigidity that were its fatal flaws.

~ David Brooks

There was, I think, never any reason to believe in the innate superiority of the male, except in his superior muscle.

~ Bertrand Russell

There are few successful adults who were not at first successful children.

~ Alexander Chase

People seem not to see that their opinion of the world is also a confession of character.

~ Ralph Waldo Emerson

Those who are faithful know only the trivial side of love; it is the faithless who know love's tragedies.

~ Oscar Wilde

It is seldom indeed that one parts on good terms, because if one were on good terms one would not part.

~ Marcel Proust

The only difference between the Democrats and the Republicans is that the Democrats allow the poor to be corrupt, too.

~ Oscar Levant

Hard work is damn near as overrated as monogamy.

~ Huey P. Long

Anybody who wants the presidency so much that he'll spend two years organizing and campaigning for it is not to be trusted with the office.

~ David Broder

Giving every man a vote has no more made men wise and free than Christianity has made them good

~ H. L. Mencken

The whole history of these books [the Gospels] is so defective and doubtful that it seems vain to attempt minute enquiry into it: and such tricks have been played with their text, and with the texts of other books relating to them, that we have a right, from that cause, to entertain much doubt about what parts of them are genuine. In the New Testament there is internal evidence that parts of it have proceeded from an extraordinary man; and that other parts are of the fabric of very inferior minds. It is as easy to separate those parts as to pick out diamonds from dunghills.

~ Thomas Jefferson

The squeaking wheel doesn't always get the grease. Sometimes it gets replaced.

~ Vic Gold

Good advice is something a man gives when he is too old to set a bad example.

~ Francois, Duc de La Rochefoucauld

A cult is a religion with no political power.

~ Tom Wolfe

Greatest fools are oft most satisfied.

~ Nicolas Boileau

Religion is less a matter of holiness than an excuse for dispute.

~ Baron de Montesquieu

Power only tires those who don't exercise it.

~ Pierre Elliott Trudeau

What is said when drunk has been thought out beforehand.

~ Flemish proverb

The only normal people are the ones you don't know very well.

~ Joe Ancis

Life will always remain a gamble, with prizes sometimes for the imprudent, and blanks so often to the wise.

~ Jerome K. Jerome

Nobody realizes that some people expend tremendous energy merely to be normal.

~ Albert Camus

Don't go around saying the world owes you a living. The world owes you nothing. It was here first.

~ Mark Twain

Speaking generally, punishment hardens and numbs, it produces concentration, it sharpens the consciousness of alienation, it strengthens the power of resistance.

~ Friedrich Nietzsche

Banking establishments are more dangerous than standing armies.

~ Thomas Jefferson

In jealousy there is more self-love than love.

~ Francois, Duc de La Rochefoucauld

I was going to have cosmetic surgery until I noticed that the doctor's office was full of portraits by Picasso.

~ Rita Rudner

If you hate a person, you hate something in him that is part of yourself. What isn't part of ourselves doesn't disturb us.

~ Herman Hesse

A temperance advocate visited Lincoln at the White House to protest the whiskey drinking of General Grant. After listening to the complaint, Lincoln said: "Find out the brand of the whiskey General Grant uses. I would like to furnish the same brand to my other generals."

~ Bill Adler

A beauty is one you notice; a charmer is one who notices you.

~ Adlai E. Stevenson

The deepest definition of youth is life as yet untouched by tragedy.

~ Alfred North Whitehead

Scoundrels are always sociable.

~ Arthur Schopenhauer

The enemies of the future are always the nicest people.

~ Christopher Morley

Say not you know another entirely, till you have divided an inheritance with him.

~ Johann Kasper Lavater

People hate those who make them feel their own inferiority.

~ Lord Chesterfield

The road up and the road down are one and the same.

~ Heraclitus

Though boys throw stones at frogs in sport, the frogs do not die in sport, but in earnest.

~ Bion

Almost all of our faults are more pardonable than the methods we resort to hide them.

~ Francois, Duc de La Rochefoucauld